The Edwin O. Reischauer Lectures, 2001

Lost Modernities

China, Vietnam, Korea,
and the Hazards of World History

Alexander Woodside

Harvard University Press

Cambridge, Massachusetts

London, England

2006

Library of Congress Cataloging-in-Publication Data

Woodside, Alexander.
Lost modernities : China, Vietnam, Korea, and the hazards of
world history / Alexander Woodside.
p. cm. — (The Edwin O. Reischauer lectures)
Includes bibliographical references and index.
ISBN 0-674-02217-3 (alk. paper)
1. Bureaucracy—China—History.   2. Bureaucracy—Vietnam—History.   3. Bureaucracy—
Korea—History.   4. China—Politics and government.   5. Vietnam—Politics and government.
6. Korea—Politics and government.   I. Title.
JQ1510.W66 2006
320.951—dc22   2005056710

For John, Mike, Melinda,
and Gloria Woodside

Contents

Preface   ix

Introduction   1

1 Questioning Mandarins   17

2 Meritocracy's Underworlds   38

3 Administrative Welfare Dreams   56

4 Mandarin Management Theorists?   77

   Conclusion   107

   Notes   119

   Index   135

Preface

The four chapters of this book were presented, in more compressed form, as the Edwin O. Reischauer Lectures for 2001 at Harvard University. The Introduction has been written more recently. I was very honored to be asked to give these lectures, and I wish to thank Professors Elizabeth Perry (who extended the invitation), Roderick MacFarquhar, Ezra Vogel, Hui-Tam Ho Tai, Philip Kuhn, Suzanne Ogden, and other colleagues in the Harvard Asian Studies community for their warm hospitality when I was briefly reunited with them.

I should also thank the John Simon Guggenheim Memorial Foundation for a grant that helped me to do some of the research and thinking that are incorporated into these chapters. I am grateful as well to the Humanities Research Centre at the Australian National University, which provided me with a most congenial research base a few years ago. Finally, I should thank my colleagues at the Institute of Asian Research at the University of British Columbia—most particularly Pitman Potter, Michael Leaf, Diana Lary, Tim Cheek, and Dan Overmyer—for the collegial and stimulating scholarly atmosphere they create. Comparative historians sometimes find themselves sharing the dilemma of the hapless Buddhist monks in medieval Chinese pornographic novels who can't make their activities seem respectable to everyone. With colleagues such as the ones I have in the Choi building, it is a pleasure to think about the comparative study of Asian civilizations.

Lost Modernities

Introduction

In this book I propose that the rationalization processes we think of as "modern" are more manifold than is often assumed. They may occur independently of one another, as a multiplicity of developments, in some instances quite separately from such obvious landmarks as the growth of capitalism or industrialization.

To defend this proposition, I reconsider one common element in the history of China, Korea, and Vietnam from the time of the Tang dynasty (618–907 C.E.) in China, including the major Korean and Vietnamese dynasties after these two smaller countries had broken away from Chinese rule. These were the Koryo (918–1392) and Choson (1392–1910) dynasties in Korea and the Ly (1010–1225), Tran (1225–1400), Le (1428–1788), and Nguyen (1802–1945) dynasties in what is now called Vietnam. (The Vietnamese did not generally call themselves "Vietnamese" before the twentieth century, any more than the "ancient Greeks" called themselves Greeks; but anachronisms cannot be avoided here.)

That common element under reconsideration is the rise of embryonic bureaucracies, based upon clear rules, whose personnel were obtained—in form at least—independently of hereditary social claims, through meritocratic civil service examinations. The notion that the basis of good politics could be established through the "development of people" (*zuo ren* in Chinese)—that is, by training people to be politically useful, rather than by taking them as they were—goes far back before the unification of China in 221 B.C.E. But it was the Tang dynasty that made success or failure in the struggle for Chinese government positions theoretically dependent upon the scrutiny of candidates' talent, by means of public competitions held at fixed periods. And it was the Tang dynasty that allowed civil service office-

1

seekers to make their own applications for advancement through examinations, rather than requiring them to get the recommendations of aristocratic patrons or high court officials.

The examination sites themselves became public spectacles. In China in the 1700s the Jiangnan examination site—a walled complex of brick huts to which individual candidates were assigned—accommodated more than sixteen thousand students. The sites reminded people of the importance of the competitive measurement of administrative talent, roughly in the way our big football stadiums remind us now of the excitement of athletic competition. The spectacular quality of the examinations was, in effect, an appeal to public opinion, an advertisement not just of the examinations' importance but also of their claim to what would now be called transparency. By the 1400s, for example, applicants' answers in the Korean civil service examinations passed through the hands of collection officers, registration officers, recording officials, collating officers, and readers, whose tasks were to see to it that candidates' names were concealed from their examiners; that their answers were recopied in other people's handwriting before examiners saw them; and that many examiners, not one, evaluated the candidates' performances. Not even the examinations at contemporary Western universities take so many transparency-enhancing precautions.

The examinations were also intensely bureaucratic, anticipating the world for which they were recruiting talent. The precolonial Vietnamese civil service examinations, which are probably the least well known of the three, demonstrated this bureaucratic flavor in the early 1800s very clearly. Usually held in fields patrolled by elephants, and full of candidates' tents (as contrasted with China's brick huts), the three-stage regional Vietnamese examinations were held on the first, sixth, and twelfth days of the seventh lunar month; the winners were publicly announced, in order of excellence, on the twenty-third day. Staff at the sites included proctors, invigilators, and preliminary, intermediate, and master examiners. All of them had to sign the examination books they processed; the 1834 regulations forbade the examiners to meet one another privately, let alone to gamble or play games, while the examinations were in progress. Quotas were set in advance for the numbers of winners permitted, and in the provinces where the examinations were held local officials had to make the special hats and clothes for their quotas of degree winners one month before the examinations began. Brothers, fathers and sons, and uncles and nephews were allowed to take the examinations together, in a suspension of Confucian family hierarchy. But examiners had to file written reports as to whether these relatives had entered the sites together, and how closely the styles of their answers coincided, in order to protect the importance of individual effort as against that of family solidarity.

In all three mandarinates rulers were nervous about the examinations' potential for literary forms of mockery or subversion, aimed at them. So there were word-count controls. In the first half of the 1800s Vietnamese examiners' questions had to obey word limits (300 words at the regional examinations for policy questions). So did candidates' answers (1,000 words for regional policy answers). Like our own contemporary civil service examinations, therefore, the preindustrial Chinese, Korean, and Vietnamese examinations could hardly be accused of stimulating pure thought. But they did prepare candidates for the stereotyped paperwork of administrators, such as the rice price reports, comparing changing rice prices in the provincial capital with the prices prevailing in a sample outlying county of the same province, that Vietnamese provincial officials had to send to the court at Hue four times a year in the early 1800s.

The examinations and the governments dependent upon them gave the preindustrial Chinese, Vietnamese, and Korean polities split personalities. Essentialist accounts of their political histories miss their precarious synthesis of incompletely compatible elements. On the one hand, there was the stress upon administrative utility, and trust in invisible, nonfamilial authority (such as that of the examiners). On the other hand, there was the faith in Confucian virtue, not utility, and the ethical supremacy not of invisible authority but of kinship hierarchies, or simulations of kinship relations. Multiple value systems, varying from individual to individual in degrees of acceptance, must have created a certain amount of normative ambivalence, even if they helped as much as hindered political stability. Yet pluralism—meaning in this instance a competitive coexistence of different values and institutions, in which none imposed itself to the complete exclusion of the others—was long thought by nineteenth-century European thinkers, ranging from Guizot to Tocqueville and beyond, to be the monopoly of what they deemed the world's only progressive civilization, that of Europe. It is no doubt excessive to write, as one British historian did, that the east Asian examinations were "forerunner to that current American obsession, the exaltation of PhD training." Yet a clarification of the place of the east Asian mandarinates in world history is nonetheless crucial to the criticism of those false forms of revolutionary fantasy that exaggerate the differences between "traditional" worlds and "modern" ones.[1]

The term "modern" was fatally compromised by its provincialism right from the outset. The term apparently emerged in late written Latin. By the ninth century Europeans were applying it to the age of Charlemagne, as a way of contrasting Charlemagne's rule in western Europe with the "antiquity" of both pagan writers and the early Church fathers. Yet compared with Charlemagne's empire, Tang dynasty China (and probably also the Cambodian Angkor empire) was at this time arguably more modern—as we would understand the term—in state capacity and political management.[2] The extreme antidote to this provincialism has been to claim, in the words of the French scholar Bruno Latour, that "we have never been modern." We falsely think we have separated Nature and Society, whereas in fact all we have done has been carelessly to "mix together much greater masses of humans and nonhumans"; our "myth of the soulless, agentless bureaucracy, like that of the pure and perfect marketplace, offers the mirror-image of the myth of universal scientific laws"; rationalization itself is at once a sin we are incapable of committing and a virtue we are incapable of possessing.[3]

The historian's halfway house between these two extremes might be to follow the lead of the legal historian Harold J. Berman. Berman's 1983 work on the formation of the Western legal tradition urged us to move "beyond Marx, beyond Weber" and to overcome the fallacies of various Western nationalisms, religious prejudices, and nineteenth-century historical materialisms and ideal-type analyses, in rewriting our past. Specifically, Berman took on both Protestants and Marxists in arguing that the modernization of Western legal systems had really begun with the papal revolution in canon law from the eleventh to the thirteenth centuries, long before capitalism or industrialism. Our overly simple genealogy of what was modern in Western history therefore needed to be revised, not least by the exercise of looking for the "modern characteristics" in "what is generally considered to be a premodern era."[4] If the Berman exercise is worth performing for Western history, it is equally worth performing for Asian history. That is the purpose of this book.

The Berman approach necessarily means disclaiming (once again) pictures of Chinese, Vietnamese, and Korean preindustrial history that have the peoples of these kingdoms "sighing and groaning" through many centuries of dynasties that "rose and fell," the "retarding force" of such monarchies and their cycles being attributed to a "sea" of "feudal" economic arrangements.[5] For contemporary Chinese political dissidents like Yan Jiaqi, whose words I have just quoted, pessimism is understandable. But history does not tyrannize by itself; it provides opportunities. A politically intelligent Martian would not have had kind words to say about the democratic potential of German history, if he had gone there in 1938, or of that of Spain if he had gone there in 1960.

Of course the mandarinates' monarchies were palpably unmodern in many ways, not least in the parasitism of their royal families, especially in China. (The Ming grand secretary Xu Guangqi calculated in the early 1600s that there were about eighty thousand living relatives of the Ming royal house that had ruled China since 1368; all of them were entitled to government stipends.)[6] Such parasitism was serious not just economically but psychologically. In China it irritated "aristogenic" civil servants who had a strong feudal nostalgia, and an injustice-collecting tendency to contrast their own inability to mobilize what they regarded as their full patrilineal kinship lines with the far greater capacity to do so of the royal house, not to mention the legendary hereditary feudal lords of a bygone age.[7] But the European state that inspired Max Weber's picture of modern bureaucratic rationalism—his own Germany of Kaiser Wilhelm II—was dominated before World War One by a monarchy and warrior caste that could equally have been described as archaic or unmodern.

Nobody captured the normative ambivalence of the credentials-worshipping mandarinates—in the form of the fury of would-be aristocrats who nonetheless had to pass examinations before they could compete for the small number of jobs in the state bureaucracy—better than the Korean reformer Yi Ik (1681–1762). His words are worth quoting, not least because they recognize the kinship of the Korean and Chinese mandarinates: "In Korea, the selection of officials is entirely based on the civil examination system . . . Ts'ui Liang of the [Chinese] Northern Wei dynasty once remarked that even with ten people sharing one office, there would still not be enough posts to go around. This remark applies very well to the current (Korean) situation. Hence, in families boasting of an aristocratic lineage or intellectual tradition, there are innumerable people, thin as rakes, clutching their credentials and giving vent to their bitter resentment."[8]

Had the east Asian mandarinates been as "feudal" as they are sometimes depicted—in the sense of having a strong hereditary correspondence or parallelism among kinship, economic rewards, and political power, extending from courts to villages—one of the central problems of their political theory, the weakness of communications between "high" and "low," or rulers and ruled, would be hard to explain. That was a bureaucratic issue:

the monarchs of the mandarinates largely governed through texts composed for them by mandarins, rather than by more personal (and perhaps more feudal) means of persuasive human contact.

The point may be demonstrated by a look at two multiethnic empires in the 1700s. The Manchu emperor Qianlong, who ruled China and also the Mongols and other central Asian peoples for most of that century, could adopt a personal and indeed feudal style with the elites he ruled outside China proper. Yet even here the culture of the mandarinate asserted itself. Qianlong complained that he personally had to correct edicts written in Beijing by his Mongol and Manchu translators because the Mongol and Manchu nobles for whom they were intended could not understand them. The breakdown was the fault of court translators, who were not Chinese themselves but had nonetheless grown up in Beijing and been influenced by Chinese examination prose mannerisms, which had spread like a virus to the other written languages of the bureaucracy. This was not the sort of problem likely to afflict the rulers of Europe's most significant multiethnic empire in the 1700s, that of the Habsburgs in Vienna. In Vienna there was no monoculture of civil service examinations. Magyar and Czech and Croat clerks were not so eager to Germanize themselves linguistically that they took up a stilted style that threatened the Habsburgs' ability to communicate with minority nobilities on their frontiers. Indeed when Qianlong's opposite number, the Habsburg archduchess Maria Theresa, wished to appeal to her Hungarian nobles to support her in a war in the 1740s, she appeared before them as a supplicant carrying the crucifix of a celebrated emperor of the previous century, plus her four-month-old baby.[9] Qianlong, in contrast, tried to restore communications with his Mongol nobles by ordering a "back to basics" reform of examination-system writing, in which examiners were to weed out "eight-legged essay" superficialities. So much for our traditional pictures of the empire of China as founded upon "face"-based relationships and "feelings," Europe as founded upon impersonal rules and reason.

The precocious limited defeudalization of the three Asian polities that had examination systems is in fact part of the history of human reason, of the attempt to apply supposedly rational thought to politics and economics. As such, the topic cannot be discussed in an entirely triumphalist manner. A different kind of history is needed, in which the focus is directed toward the vulnerabilities of this experiment as well as its achievements, the magnetism of the ideal but also the pressures over the centuries, in all three polities, to abandon it. In particular, the theme of how political systems imagine risks is critical to this form of comparative history. How did German rulers imagine political hazards after Luther? Or English property owners after the Levellers? Or how do elites in industrial societies conceptualize the hazards of global warming now? The east Asian effort to create nonhereditary merit-based power altered the way Chinese, Vietnamese, and Korean thinkers imagined risks. The effort itself was a very great "leap in the dark" (to borrow the phrase British conservative leaders used a century and a half ago to characterize the extension of voting rights), and its fears as well as its excitements need to be captured. Western thinkers like Machiavelli and Pascal saw the hazards of merit-based power almost entirely in simple terms of the resentments of the excluded; the mandarinates' political theory, for many centuries, scrutinized also the self-subversion of meritocratic elites from within.

The result is that much contemporary Western public administration theory functions like an unconscious echo chamber of questions and controversies that, in admittedly much different language, were explored in the mandarinates a long time ago. In the early twenty-first century, for example, Western specialists in public administration anxiously dissect what they call the "bureaucratic accountability paradox." Postfeudal public servants are on the one hand mere instruments of higher political authority, epitomizing as such the danger of a deficiency of personal responsibility for what they do; on the other hand they are active policymaking participants, epitomizing as such the danger of a usurpation of higher political authority by their own subjective behavior. And explicit and implicit demands for accountability within bureaucracies, designed to communicate performance standards for such officials in this type of setting, may actually weaken the individual moral capacities the officials need to obey such standards in a fully responsible manner.

East Asian mandarins, obliged to work with a more moralistic Confucian world view, discussed this problem more as a matter of the difficulty of creating greater "self-esteem" among government officials, or the difficulty of nourishing (from without) a sense of "shame" among more menial government clerks. But the rudiments of accountability paradox theory were there, by the Ming dynasty if not earlier. The problem of shamelessness in the exercise of power, within a merit-based bureaucracy, is a modern one. It is not just the quaint obsession of bygone Confucian literati. The point is not to romanticize feudalism (as many Confucian literati did), even if it may be true, as Noam Chomsky suggested some time ago, that mandarins are not always more benign than aristocrats.[10] Attempts to increase merit-based power, pioneered in eastern Asia, are nonetheless surely an advance. But fairness to the grandeur of the struggle to do this requires that we look at its hazards too.

Accordingly, in Chapter 1 of this book I introduce the three mandarinates. I argue that the Korean and Vietnamese civil service examinations, beginning in the eighth and the eleventh centuries respectively, are at least as instructive as the better-known Chinese examinations. Full political refeudalization was always more possible in the two smaller kingdoms, allowing for a greater opposition to postfeudal meritocratic ideals; yet refeudalization never entirely succeeded. In all three mandarinates, moreover, there were precocious concerns about "grade inflation" in the examinations themselves; at least the beginnings of a critical awareness of their own administrative subjectivities; a growing use of the language of administrative utility rather than a political language celebrating the virtues of hereditary privilege; and, especially in China, an anxiety about the transition, by means of the relatively anonymous examinations, from face-to-face political activity to more depersonalized modes of administrative management as the polity expanded.

In Chapter 2 I argue that the mandarinates anticipated various hazards of meritocracy that the Western experience has largely confronted more recently. These included hazards related to the instabilities of impersonal administrative power based upon written texts. They also included hazards related to postfeudal forms of elite self-esteem creation, which came less and less from within (inner satisfaction at successfully embodying heroic or aristocratic virtues) and more and more from without (in an environment where class and status ethics were no longer preordained, state techniques of encouragement such as better salaries became more important). And they included the hazard that political orders based upon merit-based bureaucracies might have a weaker capacity to mobilize their peoples for public goals than regimes based upon feudal service ethics or (in more recent times) mass patriotism.

In Chapter 3 I argue that the three mandarinates pursued welfare goals like the alleviation of poverty and the greater equalization of landholding, but that in their very modern-seeming conversion of political problems like poverty into administrative concerns, they ran the risk of allowing administrative goals to become decontextualized ends in themselves, contributing to a disjunction between administrators and administered, and to significant kinds of public apathy. All three mandarinates tried to overcome the apathy and revitalize local political behavior in acceptable ways, such as through the Neo-Confucian formula of village covenants. These are contrasted with the artificial forms of community creation of early modern Europe. Ironically, the covenants worked least well in China, whose deeper bureaucratic culture created the greatest need for them.

Chapter 4 moves from the precolonial period to the postcolonial present. In it I suggest that the continuing ghostly presence of the mandarinates in the contemporary Asian Leninist reform states of China and Vietnam lies not so much in specific institutions as in the persistence of a more general crisis (well known to the mandarins) of bureaucratic subjectivity, now greatly expanded. At the end of the twentieth century certain aspects of mandarinism were being reinvented in eastern Asia along cross-cultural or transnational lines. The danger was that centuries of skepticism about bureaucracy, than which nothing was more east Asian, would not be revived as speedily in this process. Compulsory family planning programs in contemporary China and Vietnam are used to illustrate this danger, and to show that the old incubus of bureaucratic subjectivity is now doubly determined, by domestic bureaucratic practices but also by imported global managerial theories such as cybernetics and "system engineering."

The title of this book could just as easily have been "lost creativities." Modernity (singular) is a dubious concept, as I concede in more detail in Chapter 1. A focus on modernity may oversimplify (if not suppress) historically lived time; it may ignore history's "losers," and the various modes of resistance to power, legitimate or illegitimate; and it may even indicate complicity with the workings of global capitalism. (Just what this last could exemplify in practice is the argument, in present-day China, that "mountain people" are a threat to any rational political system because large-scale capital investment in grain production in mountainous areas will yield only modest returns; and that in the name of modernity's requirement that all human societies move from a "mountain-rural" to a "plains-urban" civilization, China's "mountain people" should be forcibly resettled from mountainous areas.)[11] "Modernities" pluralized, in contrast, allows us to begin to uncover traditions of discursive rationality that the cruder singular notion of the modern has obscured; or at least to end uses of the singular term for the modern that merely camouflage one civilization's historical self-centeredness.

But how did the modernities that I propose existed in preindustrial east Asia get "lost"? For Westerners, from the second half of the 1800s on, the east Asian examinations lost their novelty, and therefore their provocativeness. In previously aristocratic European societies there was an increase in numbers of non-aristocratic civil servants; the belief grew that merit could be measured; in the 1860s the very term "meritocracy" came to be used in British Labour Party journals. In this new epoch in Western history, an epoch of IQ tests and intelligence-measurement researchers like Alfred Binet and Edward Thorndike, the more limited techniques of the older east Asian meritocracies—which (unlike the new Western merit-judging procedures) had not discriminated against old age as well as against hereditary claims—began to resemble exotic, old-fashioned relics. But it is less easy to understand why Asians themselves should have given such short shrift to their own pasts.

The loss of these modernities begins with the military defeats the French, British, and Japanese inflicted upon the three mandarinates in the 1800s. The one-sided conflict between the two technological worlds represented by steam-powered Western warships and preindustrial Chinese war junks, at the time of the Opium War, also exposed, in an unprecedentedly humiliating way, the deficits in administrative achievement about which sensitive scholar-officials had been worrying for many centuries before the industrial revolution. The weakness of all bureaucracies, not just Confucian ones, is their inability to create feelings of belonging equal to those found in the patron-client relations of the European, Japanese, and Thai feudal periods, or in the politics of states based upon mass nationalisms. A look at the troubles of the contemporary European Union will show that the problem is not a peculiarly nineteenth-century Asian one. The mandarinates' difficulties in increasing their capacities for popular mobilization for collective purposes harbored a paradox. A bureaucracy's formal ideology rarely reflects what the bureaucracy actually does. Nonetheless, the need for at least some conformity with this ideology, in the interests of idealizing the bureaucracy's public mission, not only makes changes in the ideology awkward, but awkward even to explain, to the bureaucracy's beneficiaries and dependents.

For this reason the elite government leaders who successfully proposed the abolition of China's civil service examinations in 1905—just at the moment when the Western world was beginning to embrace such examinations—did not make the actual subject matter of the examinations their principal target. The examinations could have been converted, after all, to the service of a new curriculum. What the abolitionists attacked was the Chinese examinations' association with an insufficiency of collective will-power. In 1905 Yuan Shikai and his fellow reformers asserted that Prussia's victory over France in 1871, and Japan's victory over Russia in 1905 itself, were due not to Prussian and Japanese soldiers but to the socializing force behind those two countries' soldiers, namely their primary school teach-ers. (This myth—that patriotism-inculcating schoolteachers could pro-duce military victories—was then current all over the world; in 1905 Sid-ney and Beatrice Webb, the British social reformers, were making exactly the same claim as Yuan Shikai.) The purpose of education, they insisted, must be mass mobilization, not bureaucratic recruitment. China must make a psychological revolution, shifting from a mandarinate whose edu-cational interest was "storing talent" to a more collectively minded society whose schools aroused and enlightened popular willpower.[12]

As examination-based civil services multiplied in the Western world af-ter 1905, however, the Asian mandarinates should have regained some of their historical persuasiveness. That their modernities remained "lost" may be explained by the rise and popularity, all over the world, of Western sci-entific management theory. Frederick Winslow Taylor, perhaps the most globally influential American thinker of the twentieth century, published his book on "scientific management" in 1911. Taylor claimed that only the most precise scientific methods, applied to the analyses of the relations be-tween human workers and the new industrial machinery, could increase workers' efficiency.

The effect of "Taylorism" was to spread the illusion, in World War One and its immediate aftermath, that Taylor's quasi-utopian theories of in-creased work productivity, in places like steel mills, through more "scien-tific" links between work classifications and their material rewards, could be applied to the work of civil servants as well; the techniques of getting enhanced performances from Bethlehem Steel's shovelers and iron han-dlers might be transferred to enhance the performances of government secretaries and clerks. By the end of the 1920s both the British govern-ment and the American federal government had struggled to adopt "scien-tific" systems of civil service work classifications, in which pay levels were tightly linked to work positions. This principle implied a more materialis-tic definition of civil servants' natures than that favored in the less "scien-tific" mandarinates. Material rewards were everything in Taylorism, the moral nobility of good administration far less.

Taylorist gospel inevitably spread to China. By the 1930s Nationalist

China not only had its own journals devoted to the administrative sciences, with titles like "Administration Research" and "Administrative Efficiency," but its own Administrative Efficiency Research Society (*Xingzheng xiaolü yanjiu hui*). The Nanjing government promoted the translation and introduction of European and American theories of "personnel administration." There was an elite debate over whether China should follow the British or the American approach to the classification of civil service posts; almost two millennia of Chinese bureaucratic experience were ignored. The political scientist Qian Duansheng argued for the British model, on the grounds that it was simpler than the American one; American civil service job classifications were allegedly too sophisticated and too finely differentiated to succeed in China, given what Qian thought were the cultural conservatism and the skilled reflexes of evasiveness of Chinese officialdom. Xie Bokang, whose 1937 book *Renshi xingzheng dagang* (An outline of personnel administration) was probably the most influential text of its kind in China before 1949, conceded the greater complexity of the American scheme of bureaucratic job classifications. But he demanded its application anyway, on the grounds that it better represented global developmental trends.[13] The Taylorization of bureaucracy—the recasting of bureaucracy in the image of a profit-seeking corporation—was part of the attempted "internationalization" of the Chinese government in the 1930s. The foundation for this was elite-based transnational alliances to which returned overseas students like Xie Bokang inevitably belonged.

In fact the Nationalist government largely resisted the rationalization implicit in American or British civil service rules. These were more influential, if anywhere, at the Chinese municipal level. But what is remarkable is that the presumption that bureaucracies could be made more effective through differential rewards for difficult and simple tasks completely ignored the evolution (and contestation) of this principle in the preindustrial mandarinates.

Amnesia of this sort also reigned in Vietnam, a French colony between the 1880s and 1954. The French colonizers preserved the mandarinate in the north and center of the country. But they made it humiliatingly subordinate to a better-paid French colonial bureaucracy. The French also abolished the mandarinate's competitive civil service examinations in 1919 without replacing them with an equally meritocratic new recruitment system, and they generally converted what one Vietnamese observer called this increasingly "ridiculous caricature" of a mandarinate into a pitiful symbol of Vietnamese inferiority to their European rulers. The moral ethos of the old mandarins vanished.[14]

The communist revolutions in the former mandarinates, until very recently, also worked to ensure that the history of the mandarinates remained lost. Lenin greatly admired Taylorism and American management theory. He claimed in 1918 that socialism was a matter of Soviet power, Prussian railroads, and American techniques. Stalin reinforced this message in 1924 with the proposition that the "combination of Russian revolutionary sweep and American efficiency is the essence of Leninism in party and state work."[15] It is true that for a long time communist revolutionaries condemned political science, to which much Western postwar thinking about bureaucracy belonged, as a "capitalist class science"; but they eventually relented, with Yugoslavia relegitimizing the study of political science in 1951, Czechoslovakia in 1965, Rumania in 1969, China in the early 1980s, and Vietnam, most belatedly, in 1991. Behind this reinstatement lurked the belief that if power produced knowledge, the relationship between the two could be reversed: the Asian acquisition of Western knowledge about bureaucracy would facilitate the acquisition of Asian administrative power of a quality comparable to that of the mature Western industrial states. In other words, the loss of the history of the mandarinates' modernities seemed a necessary accompaniment of the hope of convergence.

Of course the reluctance of the descendants of the mandarinates to recognize their achievement, indeed the double damnation of the mandarinates for being both tools of "despotism" and arenas of pre-Taylorist "inefficiency," has its funny side. When the Chinese leader Zhu Rongji congratulated some Chinese scientists in 1996 for founding a management sciences department, he urged them to expand their study of Western management science, singling out for praise Lee Iacocca's reorganization of the Chrysler automobile corporation. Zhu conceded in passing that preindustrial China had also produced good management thought; but the examples he gave (Guanzi, the Han dynasty "salt and iron" debate) all safely preceded the full decline of the Chinese aristocratic age. Taiwanese Chinese disciples of the Austrian economist Friedrich von Hayek—who argued that most forms of equality were inimical to liberty, and that the hereditary transmission of property and power strengthened the social good—have gone even farther. They have praised the aristocratic world of Confucius, about a millennium before the consolidation of civil service examinations, as the best evidence of Hayek-style enlightenment in Chinese history, before the shabby limited egalitarianism of the meritocratic ideal took root.

Contemporary Chinese critics of bureaucracy dismiss the British historian Arnold Toynbee's claim that England borrowed its modern civil service from China. As one of them put it recently (in 2000), any Chinese person who celebrates this is "an Ah Q": a reference to the novelist Lu Xun's famous character, a feckless villager with bogus self-esteem who depends upon fantasizing about victories that are really defeats. In Vietnam one psychologist at the end of the 1970s felt the need to point out publicly that even Hanoi newspaper cartoons about Vietnamese bureaucrats were cut off from history. They surrounded their subjects with Western office paraphernalia that Vietnamese officials did not yet possess.[16]

Such dismissals of the mandarinates' achievement possibly exist in direct proportion to a subconscious fear of it. That is, the fear that the history of the mandarinates, taken seriously and applied to present-day concerns, will remind us only too well that there is no such thing as a bureaucracy based upon pure reason. Western writings about bureaucracy, perhaps because of their relative newness as a genre, often cultivate a formalistic clarity, a disembodied normativeness, at the costs of overestimating the technical aspects of administrative behavior and underestimating the nontechnical ones. The very formalism of such writings makes it easier for contemporary eastern Asians to turn them into political cookbooks for imagining more efficient, more abstract bureaucracies than ever existed in real life, in the mandarinates or anywhere else.

No such transmutation could ever occur with the great analyses of actual bureaucratic activity written in the mandarinates, for example Wang Huizu's *Xuezhi yishuo* (Opinions about learning to govern, 1793). In Wang's text, written by a working county magistrate, officials like county magistrates live in a metaphorical wonderland. Wang compares them to medicine men, or to wooden puppets, or to glass screens. Such shifting identities, so remote from the abstract clarity of a Max Weber or a Chester Barnard, reflected the uncertainties of a postfeudal administration, easily penetrated by its environment, without a strong sense of being religiously or socially underwritten. English justices of the peace of this period could hardly have been treated in the same way. But Wang's images also point to the vulnerabilities, the messy bargaining, and the absence of clear models of action, that probably afflict bureaucratic decisionmaking in general.

This is not a popular theme in the former mandarinates in the early twenty-first century, searching as their leaders are for elixirs of self-strengthening.

Obviously this book is too small to do as conclusively for the three mandarinates what Harold Berman did for the history of the Western legal tradition. That is, to demonstrate the modern characteristics in a supposedly premodern era; document the abundance of resources of human rationality in state building that existed before the Renaissance or the Enlightenment; and prove that modernizing developments, in something like law, could occur quite independently of capitalism and industrialization, as well as at their own rates. But I hope this book will incline us more to the possibility that the mandarinates were dealing with tasks and hazards of governance that were unmistakably modern, rather than just those of preindustrial "despotisms" whose independence was jeopardized in the 1800s.

The study of the mandarinates' political and administrative theory, in particular, should not be entirely shoved aside by our interest in their varying aptitudes for capitalism, or in their Confucian ethics and ritual conditioning processes. As to the latter, the Mussolini formula ("moral order" produces "public order," the Italian dictator famously maintained) is as much wishful thinking as historical fact.[17] Public order depends as much upon political activity and its theorizations as it does upon social "orthopraxy."

I hope this book will also call attention to the transnational nature of the three Asian mandarinates and the ways in which their different experiences illuminate one another. To this end, China, Vietnam, and Korea all feature in the story. This approach may confound readers who are used to distinguishing between "East Asia" (China, Japan, and Korea) and "Southeast Asia" (Vietnam and its neighbors to the west and south). But the terms "East Asia" and "Southeast Asia" are idols of the postwar Western academic (and strategic) mind. Up to a point they are useful for carving up subject matter at our universities. But they should not be allowed to paralyze intellectual inquiry. I am not pleading for the complete disestablishment of such categories, merely for a less reverential attitude toward them. After all, the day may even come when we may want to compare the histories of Korea and Burma, making the impact of Buddhism the unifying principle.

However: I am not a Korean studies specialist. The field of Korean studies is more of a battleground than most. Yet I suspect that even the most quarrelsome scholars in Korean studies would muster a rare degree of collective agreement among themselves that outsiders such as myself were unfit to generalize about Korean history. Readers should therefore be aware that what is said about Korea in the following pages is even less authoritative than what is said about China and Vietnam.

— 1 —

Questioning Mandarins

In the preface to his global history of the last thousand years, Felipe Fernandez-Armesto writes that he has a vision of a galactic museum of the distant future; in this museum, Diet Coke cans will share space with medieval coats of chain mail, in a single small glass showcase marked "Planet Earth, 1000–2000: The Christian Era."[1] If we were to make this glass showcase less Eurocentric, and expand it at least to commemorate the artifacts of the Christian-Confucian era between 1000 and 2000 c.e., we would surely add an east Asian civil service examination book to the chain mail and the Diet Coke cans.

The history of the three mandarinates of China, Vietnam, and Korea offers a challenge to global historians that they have yet to address satisfactorily. The term "mandarinates" here does not just mean bureaucracies based upon limited terms of office and personnel evaluations by superiors, although east Asia pioneered such forms of rule. It also means political systems, based upon the world's earliest civil service tests, which Confucian scholar-officials administered, and in which there was a centuries-long struggle to exemplify in practice what was still only an ideal for nineteenth-century European liberals like Matthew Arnold or Wilhelm von Humboldt: an education-based government of talents.

The Chinese philosopher Zhu Xi (1130–1200) compared the scholarly skills of thorough reading to the skills of patient tax collecting. Such an extraordinary association of these two things would surely not have occurred anywhere outside east Asia in the twelfth century, and it captures the peculiar flavor of the mandarinates. That there are no relics of the mandarinates in Fernandez-Armesto's galactic museum suggests that we need to look at the inclusionary and exclusionary practices in the stories we tell

17

ourselves about how we became modern. This is particularly true of those stories that transcend the history of capitalism and allow for the possibility that rationalization processes may occur in different social realms independently of one another, and at their own rates.

Immanuel Wallerstein has usefully suggested that what the West currently regards as modernity really embraces two quite different projects. The first one is the supposed triumph of humankind over nature, through the promotion of technological innovations. The second one is the triumph of humankind over itself, or at least over oppressive forms of human privilege and authority, through successful resistance to political tyranny, clerical bigotry, and economic servitude. As Wallerstein sees it, these two quests, technological and libertarian, made a "symbiotic pair" that long appeared, misleadingly, to be compatible with each other. (Galileo, after all, was thought to be fighting for both technical progress and human liberation.) But they may not, in the long run, be nearly as symbiotic or as harmonious with each other as they first seemed.[2]

Surely modernity also involves a third project, or even what Harold Perkin has dramatized as the world's "third revolution," after the first revolution (of the rise of settled farming with food surpluses) and the second revolution (of the rise of industry). That third modernity is the replacement of aristocracies by professional elites who are not necessarily either landowners or capitalists, but are knowledge-commanding professional officials, whose hierarchies are created by public competition as much as by social class.[3] This third attempted achievement of modernity, in the way it interacts with Wallerstein's first two, undoubtedly has a great deal to do with just how much increases in the uses of technology help or frustrate the dream of freedom. The preindustrial east Asian mandarinates hardly exemplified all of the characteristics of Harold Perkin's "professional classes." But they anticipated enough of them to raise questions about the narrowness of genealogies of the modern that omit them.

The weaknesses of Max Weber's famous interpretation of bureaucratic state formation, and of the passage of national power to a professional civil service, were exposed long ago by an eminent historian of Russia, Richard Pipes. Weber, in Pipes's view, feared bureaucracy too much: he exaggerated its capacity to marginalize tradition and ideology and mass psychology, and exaggerated also its capacity to block fundamental political changes once it became established.[4] But if such criticism is fair, it might be said that Weber's premonition of bureaucrats as the ultimate history-terminat-

ing interest group reflected the relative shortness of the German bureaucratic experience.

Yet Weber's general pessimism did have east Asian antecedents. The decline of the ascribed political entitlements of hereditary social hierarchies
was at best only a narrow victory for human rights, given the new bureaucratic elites' capacities for social exploitation of their own. The history of
competition-based professional bureaucracies inspired pessimism in preindustrial east Asian thinkers too, even if they were more accustomed to
the claims of bureaucracy than Weber and less haunted by the anxieties
generated by linear theories of progress. In the seventeenth century Lu
Shiyi, a remarkably acute Chinese thinker, argued that both feudal and bureaucratic systems created "impediments" to proper moral action. Feudalism's unfair distribution of rewards, and its victimization of worthy people
who were remote from the core aristocracy, were matched by bureaucracy's
declining mastery of military power and its tendency to create larger numbers of senior officials than efficiency required.[5] The east Asian examinations themselves bred controversies with an easily recognizable modern
flavor, such as those over various forms of "grade inflation." Pak Chega, an
eighteenth-century Korean diplomat, denounced Korea's excessive numbers of examinations as a bloated "lottery" that would produce far more
candidates for public office than the government needed; Vietnamese
scholars condemned the sale of access to the examinations in north Vietnam in the 1700s to merchants, peddlers, and meat shop owners, in crowds
so large that they fought with one another to enter the examination sites.[6]

Moreover, east Asian public philosophers feared that the pure utility
and the superficial, calculating behavior of the competitive examinations
would erode the moral bases of the political life they foreshadowed. In a
sort of historical doublethink, such philosophers had to remoralize that
life by all the more closely identifying it with the distant memory of the
Confucian "gentleman" of the feudal period before examinations. Ignoring
the discrepancy between the "gentleman's" seemingly anachronistic feudal
virtues and the meat shop owners then fighting for access to the civil service tests, the mandarin Le Quy Don told Vietnamese audiences in the
1700s that the "gentleman" must separate his political ambitions from
greed and desire, and "calmly" wait for the "handle" of power to pass "nat-
urally" to him after his virtue and experience had both been established in
the eyes of "court" and "country."[7] The repressed contradictions in this
thought and its context suggest that the price of the precocious early dis-

placement of even a small part of the principle of aristocracy in eastern Asia had to be the pretense that the relationship of politics to interests, let alone interest groups, could be sublimated.

If we were to put it in teleological terms that good historians would normally disavow, the east Asian quest for merit-based bureaucracy fell short of its emancipatory potential, at least as judged by later standards. In that respect it is comparable to other historical enterprises with more potential than they achieved, such as the German (Lutheran) Reformation. The comparison can be extended: fear of disorder from below, in the mandarinates as among the Germans, accompanied the decline of aristocratic authority. And just as the American and French revolutions had to make the emancipatory breakthrough that the disorder-fearing post-Reformation Germans missed, it was nineteenth-century England—according to a contemporary Chinese personnel ministry expert, writing in 1997—that began to perfect the competitive meritocracy to which the east Asian mandarinates had pointed.[8]

This sense that outsiders could redeem the promises of the east Asian past may partly explain why east Asian thought at the end of the twentieth century, far from challenging the foundationalism of Western Enlightenment rationalism, gives it a salvationist flavor. Here Enlightenment rationalism has a very broad application. It includes contemporary derivatives of itself such as the cybernetics-flavored systems theory and "system engineering," with its language of feedbacks, of inputs and outputs, of holistic control, that has become the dominant mode of Chinese elite thought since 1980, if one Chinese philosopher is to be believed.[9] The three mandarinates embodied an earlier, less technocratic search for administrative ideas that could construct a more satisfactory reality. Unlike many of the prophets of systems theory, however, their thinkers had a recurrent awareness that the real world would never completely identify itself with these ideas. Administrative planning would always produce unintended consequences. Their critical awareness about their own bureaucratic subjectivity constitutes part of their lost modernity, perhaps as much as their civil service examinations do. For many centuries, east Asian scholar officials warned that bureaucracies had a tendency to substitute texts for lived experiences, creating situations in which the "written" was totally present and the "real" or the "practical" was absent. Here was one important non-European source of the modern reflex of creative skepticism: that is, the fear of administratively produced environments that, in the name of satisfying human needs, falsified them or degenerated into demonic parodies of them.

Contemporary east Asian societies are forced to rediscover this skeptical reflex. In part this is due to their preservation of what Philip Kuhn has aptly analyzed (for China) as a "state agenda" that continues from past to present.[10] In 1998 He Qinglian, a Chinese critic of China's contemporary reforms, denounced reform officials for applying the theoretical vocabulary of Western economics to Chinese institutions without a sufficient empirical awareness of Chinese circumstances, or indeed a sufficient awareness that China's problems were larger than the "purely economic ones" to which Western economists confined themselves.[11] Her attack upon a bureaucratic policy language that separated "concepts" from real institutions because of its imaginary identification with Western economics had a long spiritual prehistory, even if its concern with the subjectivity of bureaucratic language was as much a situational continuity as a cultural one. In perhaps no other civilization could fears about a leap into a foreign cultural universe through the adoption of its vocabulary coincide so closely with centuries of elite anxiety about administrative textualizations of reality that concealed the gap between knowledge and action, the written and the practical. The conceptual isolation of a Eurocentrically defined modernity from anything in preindustrial east Asian politics obscures such continuities.

The Importance of Vietnam and Korea

The mandarinates were a cross-cultural enterprise. Their development mobilized Vietnamese and Korean energies as well as Chinese ones. Difficult as it is, they need to be represented, and imagined, pluralistically. Their diversity is to be found in their existence both as historical products and as ideal forms. Belief in the necessity of mandarins, as an ideal form, created useful psychological boundaries between the mandarinates and societies without mandarins. Korean visitors to Japan largely if not unanimously deplored Japan's lack of an examination system, not to mention the lower status of Confucian scholars in Japan's warrior culture, as compared with soldiers, doctors, or monks. Vietnamese poetry of the fifteenth and sixteenth centuries celebrated the uniquely heroic qualities of the postfeudal mandarin: such scholar-officials were represented as being like betel palms (incapable of being blown down in the wind), or like coconuts (whose juices, like mandarins' writings, allegedly quenched the people's thirst), or even like watermelons (whose red cores and green skins symbolized the scholar-official's steadfastness and material generosity).[12]

Such inflations of the postfeudal mandarin ideal were, of course, political, like inflations of the ideal of democracy in our era. And like the ideal of democracy, the ideal of the mandarin could be used to underwrite imperial expansion. In China some writers during the Qing dynasty (1644–1911) complacently compared their empire's eviction of hereditary ethnic minority chiefs in the southwest in the 1700s, by circulating bureaucrats, to the elimination of aristocratic power-holders in metropolitan China itself almost twenty centuries earlier. In this way the beginning of the end of the aristocracy in China in 221 B.C.E. became, in later centuries, a fantasy that could be projected onto the colonization of distant non-Chinese peoples like the Tai or Hmong or Yi (Lolo) as they fell within Beijing's power. Similarly, in the 1800s Beijing proconsuls in northwest China like Zuo Zongtang argued that lawless Muslim (Hui) students in China's border province of Gansu could be persuaded to give up their "Arabic" customs if the possibility of gaining "unexpected honor and good fortune" in the empire-wide civil service examinations could be held out to them.[13]

The ideal of mandarinization also facilitated the reproduction of an imperial political identity in Vietnam. In 1838 the ruler of Vietnam used local scholars in the minority areas of the Vietnamese north to spread "Han customs" (by which he meant the written culture of the Vietnamese mandarinate, not ethnic Chinese culture) among non-Vietnamese hill peoples, as part of an effort to introduce circulating bureaucrats. The same Vietnamese ruler rebuked diplomats from Siam—a country governed not by paid officials but by an intermarriage-based network of royal and noble families, who "ate" the assets of their governed areas rather than receiving salaries—for not understanding the mandarinal principle of administratively fine-tuning tax-collection levels in their country at times of natural disaster.[14]

The strength of the ideal of the scholar-official, moreover, seems to have existed somewhat independently of the huge differences in the depth of the Confucian conditioning that Korean, Chinese, and Vietnamese educational institutions offered. The Confucian academy (Chinese: *shuyuan;* Korean: *sowon*) was at least potentially one of the most important agencies of such conditioning outside the family. By the 1700s Choson Korea, with a population of perhaps seven to eight million people, had more than six hundred such academies; Qing dynasty China, with a population perhaps thirty times the size of Korea's in the eighteenth century, had little more than three times the number of Korea's academies (about nineteen hundred).[15] Vietnam, with a probable population of four to five million people at the end of the 1700s, had no real tradition of academies at all. There the task of Confucian conditioning fell mostly upon village schools and village "orthodox culture" *(tu van)* associations, composed of the village's civil service examination degree-holders; not all villages had them. Korea's superiority to China, let alone Vietnam, in the density of its academies may help to explain why polls taken even now, by east Asians themselves, show a greater predisposition to Confucian principles in Korea than in China;[16] but the general vitality of the mandarin ideal was probably unaffected by it.

As historical products, the three mandarinates were mixed systems. Obviously feudal elements (hereditary monarchs, slaves) coexisted with the pursuit of an elite meritocracy through examinations. In this respect they can be compared to polities elsewhere with split personalities, like the Western countries that for a long time combined doctrines of universal rights with institutionalized racial prejudice. All three mandarinates entertained a strong nostalgia for a more feudal society in which there were stricter, more comfortable consistencies of social status with political position and military power. (The eighteenth-century Chinese historian Wang Mingsheng characterized the uncertainty-free feudal society in revealingly archaic terms as one in which the Son of Heaven commanded ten thousand war chariots, the hereditary princes commanded one thousand war chariots, and the hereditary great officers commanded one hundred war chariots.) One of the three mandarinates, Korea, went beyond nostalgia. It came close to achieving what James Palais has somewhat controversially called an "equilibrium" between bureaucracy and aristocracy.[17] To adapt Jean Cocteau's facetious definition of the French (as being just Italians in a bad mood), it could be said that the Chinese and Vietnamese were Koreans in a less aristocratic mood.

But slaveholding in ancient Athens did not impede thousands of years of Western interest in the relevance to us of Athenian ideas of democracy. The incompleteness and corruptions of the principle of meritocracy in the three east Asian mandarinates should not be allowed to obstruct appreciation of those societies' embryonic ideas about merit-based power and their precociously administrative theories of politics. The greater difficulty lies in finding satisfactorily flexible strategies for the comparison of China, Vietnam, and Korea.

Care must be exercised with the very notion of "east Asia." There are no hermetically sealed civilizational zones. China's relations with central Asia, Korea's with northeast Asia, and Vietnam's with what we now call Southeast Asia all remained crucial. Vietnamese place names illustrate the point, such as the names of some of the most important Vietnamese cities south of the Red River delta. Da Nang is probably a Vietnamese transcription of a Cham name, preserving the memory of the old Hinduized kingdom of Champa in what is now central Vietnam; Saigon (officially Ho Chi Minh City since 1975) is probably a Vietnamese transcription of a Khmer place name (although there are other theories); and Hue may well take its name from foreign traders' mispronunciations, centuries ago, of the second word in the name of its Vietnamese prefecture Thuan Hoa.

Nor is the degree of Vietnam's historic openness to civilizations other than the Confucian mandarin one merely a matter for scholars. More general understandings of the contested identity of the contemporary Vietnamese state are at stake. Are there many Vietnams, or only one? In 1991 a Ho Chi Minh City social scientist criticized the Hanoi government for not acknowledging the Vietnamese south's stronger tradition of interaction with Southeast Asian and Pacific ocean cultures, and for not trying harder to re-create the intelligentsias of the Cham and Cambodian peoples who live in the Vietnamese south. The critic implied that the excessively assimilationist tendencies of the old Vietnamese mandarinate and its northern communist successors accounted for the shortcoming that the south (as of 1991) had no Cham studies or Khmer studies institutes.[18]

The three mandarinates still form a political and religious world, sharing common forms of Mahayana Buddhism as well as Confucianism. Both Korea and (northern) Vietnam became colonies of the Chinese Han empire in the second century B.C.E. Eight centuries later, before the two countries broke away from what was now the Chinese Tang empire, Tang China's rulers knew Korea as their "Pacified East" (*Andong*) protectorate and Vietnam as their "Pacified South" (*Annan*) protectorate. Korean and Vietnamese students at that time found educational homes in the Tang empire's capital as readily as Indian intellectuals in the twentieth century found such homes in London. In their subsequent centuries of independence, both Koreans and Vietnamese used Chinese writing, supplemented by indigenous writing systems of their own. They based their political systems upon a mixture of law—with law codes at least generally inspired by the Chinese legal tradition—and Confucian ethics, especially the ethical obligations of the hierarchical relationships known in all three countries as the "three bonds" (Chinese: *san gang;* Korean: *sam gang;* Vietnamese: *tam cuong*—the submission of subjects, children, and wives to rulers, parents, and husbands).

More particularly, by no later than the fifteenth century Vietnamese rulers had joined Chinese and Korean ones in organizing their central administrations around six specialized ministries. These ministries divided government into matters of personnel and appointments; finance and taxes; rites and education; war; justice and punishment; and public works. The family resemblance of these six ministries in Seoul, Beijing, and Thanglong (Hanoi) can be traced back to the six divisions of administration outlined in a classical text about government organization that was possibly written before the unification of the Chinese empire in 221 B.C.E.: the *Zhou li* (Rituals of Zhou).[19] The common classical tradition also meant a shared reverence for factual narrative history with moral lessons, of the sort associated with Confucius, and a shared fondness for the court centralization of historical memory. Korean and Vietnamese courts, for example, adopted the Chinese practice of compiling "veritable records" (Chinese: *shilu;* Korean: *sillok;* Vietnamese: *thuc luc*) of government business, often on a daily basis, such as could be used later for the composition of dynastic histories. Korea's Koryo dynasty (918–1392) produced its own "veritable records" before it collapsed in the fourteenth century; the earliest surviving Vietnamese version of the genre, about the uprising that created Vietnam's Le dynasty (1428–1788), appeared in the fifteenth century.

None of this meant that Vietnamese and Koreans were not independent actors; their shared world has to be put in its global context. With the strategies of state formation and of political criticism that it incorporated, the Han-Tang colonial legacy was itself pluralistic: it involved multiple, sometimes conflicting classical ideals, allowing for considerable choice. In Vietnamese and Korean eyes, these ideals and choices existed independently of any perceived ethnic Chinese proprietorship of them. Had a strong Roman empire survived for another fifteen hundred years, rather than decaying irretrievably and dividing into two distinct parts at the end of the fourth century C.E., the history of modern European countries might well have looked more like Korean and Vietnamese history in continuing to follow the political inspirations made available by the one imperial center; even so, Roman law continued to influence them. We could go even further. Until the European Renaissance, the empire of China led the world in science and technology. As it was the world's biggest single political unit, its political capacities also exceeded standards of development elsewhere. Had global communications been as efficient in the eleventh century as they are now, Europeans would have had little choice but to master Chinese political and economic theory with the same attentiveness that east Asian intellectuals now devote to the thought of American business school oracles. The Holy Roman Empire would have required at least one Wang Anshi think tank to prevent itself from falling behind global standards of organizational thought.

Civil service examinations of some sort were in existence by the seventh century in China, and by the end of the eighth and the eleventh centuries respectively in Korea and Vietnam. Modern historians of the examinations have shown some confusion as to whether they were a cause or just a consequence of the decline of hereditary aristocrats' power in the Chinese empire. Some very distinguished twentieth-century Chinese historians have argued that the explanation for the embryonic emergence of an examinations-based meritocracy in Tang China lies in the desire of the Tang rulers to strengthen their own positions at the expense of regional magnates and aristocratic power blocs. In one such formula, the Tang empress Wu, in the late seventh century, is said to have promoted palace examinations and their "presented scholar" degree (Chinese: *jinshi*; Korean: *chinsa*; Vietnamese: *tien si*), both later adopted in Korea and Vietnam, in order to create a "new social stratum" that would be dependent on her, and would offset her aristocratic foes in places like Shandong.[20]

Again, the global context is needed to see the inadequacy of such an explanation. (Purely in terms of Chinese history, it probably exaggerates the distinction between aristocrats and examination candidates in seventh-century China, and the numbers of officials who got their positions through examinations.) Power struggles between monarchs and their aristocracies or nobilities are universal. But preindustrial civil service examinations are unique to eastern Asia. Surely the standard stratagem for monarchs who wished to augment their political support, such as the rulers of Europe in the 1500s and 1600s, was simply to multiply (or adulterate) the ranks of their nobilities, by the creation of new nobles through the sale of royal letters granting noble status or the conferring of noble status as a corollary of service to the state. The first Stuart king of England tripled the number of English knights in the first two years of his reign; Queen Christina of Sweden doubled the number of Swedish noble families in just one decade.[21] We have to ask why the rulers of the east Asian mandarinates, who also at times issued non-imperial noble titles to successful royal servants, could not have survived entirely by following the Queen Christina pattern of manipulative nobility creation. Something more lies behind the invention of examinations.

The birth of Athenian democracy, seen by some as the beginning of the politically modern in the West, was brought about—scholars have suggested—not just by the residual appeal of the Greek democratic idea, but by the expansion of the Athenian empire. The empire's tasks, especially those connected to its naval ambitions, overwhelmed the existing Athenian oligarchy and compelled it to share its power with commoners.[22] On a far larger scale, something like this argument might be applied to China in the thousand years after the extraordinary feat of China's political unification. The appeal of the preimperial east Asian ideal of the search for political worthies slowly became institutionalized in written examinations as the sheer magnitude of the tasks of ruling such a huge polity, or aspiring to rule it, and the magnitude of the difficulty of preserving its unity even at the elite level, overwhelmed the capacity of any conceivable form of purely hereditary power. The examinations created the necessary new reflexes of political attachment, over such a vast space, in a way that the officials of the contemporary European Union might well envy.

But if the politics of geographical scale are part of the explanation, the Korean and Vietnamese historical experiences may be even more instructive than that of China. The Vietnamese and Korean kingdoms, being the size of Chinese provinces, were not so large that they could not be governed by hereditary power. They had less of a functional need for civil service examinations. Both Korea and Vietnam therefore had to accommodate a more acute tension between the magnetism of the meritocratic idea and the temptations of social and political refeudalization.

Korean history is the better-known example. Choson Korea's *yangban* literati families, marrying only among themselves and living in segregation from commoners in separate villages or urban quarters, resembled the Zhou feudal aristocracy of preimperial China more closely than did the more insecure, stipend-collecting scholar-officials of Ming-Qing China. Their power was such that the Korean kings remained far more modest, symbolically, than their Chinese or even their Vietnamese counterparts;

Chong Yagyong (1762–1836), one of Korea's most important political thinkers, could even imagine his king as being no more than the lead dancer in a troupe of dancers, replaceable by another member of the troupe if he did not set the right pace.[23] Martina Deuchler has cogently explored the "vast difference" between the survival of a "strong aristocratic element" in Korean life and its failure to survive so well in China, so that members of the Korean elite were encouraged to use the more nostalgically feudal side of Neo-Confucian ideology as a buttress for their hereditary power, minimizing the more egalitarian implications of that ideology as they did so.[24]

Nevertheless, even Korea's attempted neofeudal restorations were significantly incomplete. The attractiveness of the belief in merit-based achievement remained strong enough to hover over the *yangban* elite, who still had to compete for government positions through examinations. In a sharp difference from China and Vietnam, Korea, between the eleventh and the eighteenth centuries (like the pre-1860 American South), enslaved about one-third of its population. But the persuasive presence of an examination system may have at least prevented something like the old Western Aristotelian view of slaves—that there are people who are slaves by nature, for whom slavery is agreeable and just—from ever irrevocably establishing itself. When Korean slavery finally began to decline, one major Korean reformer, Yi Ik (1681–1763) demanded that the Korean government itself pay for the liberation of all slaves who could pass the civil service examinations.[25]

Vietnam—or "Annam" as the Chinese persisted in calling it down to the 1800s, rather as if the British were to continue to refer to Zimbabwe as "Rhodesia" for the next thousand years—gives us another chance to study the lure of refeudalization in a smaller mandarinate. In contrast to Korea, a peninsula whose northern frontier along the Yalu and Tumen rivers was made reasonably secure by the early 1400s, Vietnam's long open frontier with the Chams, the Khmers, the Lao, and the Tai was not fully defined before 1802. That frontier's greater openness, and the greater difficulty of establishing and consolidating land claims, worked against the maturation of hereditary power of the Korean *yangban* kind. Before the late 1400s, Vietnam probably did not yet have a distinctive scholar-official class of the Chinese type so much as a small number of talented commoners who were adjuncts of the royal aristocracy. Yet the multipolar competitiveness of the southeast Asian region in which Vietnamese rulers found themselves made the moral self-assurance of the learned mandarin ideal attractive as a weapon in dealing with non-Confucian neighbors. It was a Vietnamese mandarin diplomat, Doan Nhu Hai, who anticipated Lord Macartney by refusing to prostrate himself before the king of Hinduized Champa in the fourteenth century.

Even so, in Vietnam between the early 1500s and 1802, as in Choson Korea but not as in Ming-Qing China, the ruler's authority was limited. In those centuries the emperors of the Vietnamese Le dynasty had to share power, not with an entrenched *yangban* elite, but with a series of hereditary regional lords, like the Trinh and the Nguyen, who governed northern and southern Vietnam respectively. (Europeans called these two regions "Tonkin" and "Cochinchina.") In this period there was a remarkable de-bureaucratization or implosion of Vietnam's Red River valley mandarinate. Only one of its six ministries (the ministry of rites, which conducted the civil service examinations) kept its own public office; the other five ministries used the private households of the officials who headed them as sites for their business, meaning the privatization of their archives. After 1718 the Trinh lords even had their own rival shadow six ministries, the "six duty groups." A distinguished Japanese historian of Vietnam has proposed that these developments make the comparative study of Japan and Vietnam before 1800 inviting. Both countries had what he called "dualistic" political systems: the divided rule of emperors and shoguns in Japan, and the split authority of the emperors and the regional lords *(chua)* in Vietnam.[26]

The better comparison, however, remains the Vietnamese one with Korea. The Tokugawa shoguns could go so far as to entertain suggestions that the Japanese emperor be treated entirely as a Shinto priest and moved to the Ise religious shrine.[27] The Vietnamese ruler, like the Chinese one, could never be totally displaced from politics and transposed imaginatively to an entirely ethico-religious realm. Nor could the Vietnamese regional lords successfully develop a feudal command system based on strong personal allegiances, as could the Japanese shoguns. The spirit of the examinations-based polity, in which feudal forms of loyalty were more qualified than in Japan, could not be dispelled. So it probably makes more sense to see the hereditary regional lords of north and south Vietnam, from the 1500s to the 1700s, as representing a limited bipolar feudal restoration within an examination-system polity, a lesser version of Korea's more pervasive limited feudal restoration featuring the *yangban*.

But the meritocratic ideal never lost its latent capacity to circumscribe feudalism, even in the centuries when "dualism" covered a failure to straddle the chasm between material practices and unaffordable symbolism. One mechanism of the mandarinates for establishing government services as a public good and restricting aristocratic claims—the mechanism of rating officials in office on the quality of their performance, at fixed periods—made its nominal first appearance at Vietnamese courts by the second half of the twelfth century. (Han dynasty China had pioneered this system for rating bureaucratic performance.) The ruling class of Vietnam at that time may have been an aristocracy. But it was still subject in theory to tests of bureaucratic performance, even if these seemed so politically and socially uncomfortable and unnatural that they were carried out, if at all, only once every fifteen years. Then came Vietnam's administrative makeover of the late 1400s, which ensured the importance in Vietnamese life of state formation as seen in essentially mandarinal and bureaucratic terms. After 1471, Vietnamese officials were supposedly to be rated, and promoted or demoted, every three years, not every fifteen. The "love" of the peasants they governed was now to be measured and quantified for the court by statistical reports that counted how many peasants had fled their jurisdictions. This principle that political obedience was based, not on a feudal loyalty ethic, but upon achievement incentives such as timed promotions or demotions and money rewards or fines, was again eroded in Vietnam between 1500 and 1800. But it was not destroyed. The notion of merit had an historic vision behind it; clientelism could not match it.

Consequently the great nineteenth-century Vietnamese political thinker Phan Huy Chu (1782–1840), in the big compendium of Vietnamese history and political commentary that he wrote between 1809 and 1819, could see the whole history of Vietnamese politics, disordered as it was, as that of a quest for an objective structure of offices and laws that existed relatively independently of any particular dynasty or ruler. What animated this structure was the long effort to discover an ideal standard of administrative time control—fifteen years? nine years? three years?—that could fairly identify talent-based behavior, in whomever it was embodied, and block official corruption through the proper time cycles of personnel evaluation.[28] Rudely removed from practice as this political narrative might often be, the struggle to explore it could not be suppressed.

A society that tries to make time-based performance criteria, not just exalted social origin, the touchstone of good government has already significantly narrowed the distance between itself and the more depersonalized governance forms of the modern world. Even Vietnam, six centuries ago, drawing upon a repertoire also familiar in Chinese and Korean politics, was anticipating the psychological bases of the governance of, for example, modern universities (temporal cycles of tenure achievement and promotion) or business corporations (timed promotions and grantings of stock options). It has been said that thirteenth-century Europe began to witness the supersession of God's time by the humanly calculated time scales of traders.[29] It could be added that the supersession of natural time by bureaucratic time had also begun in the mandarinates, pluralistic as they were, and not excluding those polities small enough for refeudalization to continue to seem a realistic option. Twentieth-century Vietnamese propagandists, in articles about "the Vietnamese soul" for mass-organization newspapers, boasted that the traditional Vietnamese word for "I" *(toi)* lacked any of the individualistic force of European language words for "I" or for the self, conveying instead the pure idea of "servant" of the ruler and of his people.[30] But in Vietnam, for centuries, there was also an acceptance in theory of the existence of an individual bureaucratic "self" whose behavior was molded by administrative time cycles, a self that was not therefore entirely identical to the more idealized communitarian self of lineage and village solidarity. In all the mandarinates the simultaneous political availability of the meritocratic individual self and the more feudal communitarian self was probably a source of creative self-awareness, even if the two selves seemed contradictory.

What Time Is East Asia?

The management of time is also an important touchstone of effective comparative history. The problem of acknowledging the long existence of these partly postfeudal bureaucratic elites in China, Korea, and Vietnam, in writing world history, involves the re-creation of historical time. The more complex the world history, the more stratified its overlapping appreciations of time are likely to become.[31] If, as some philosophers contend, the problem of time is the hardest one in metaphysics, it may be the most difficult one for historians as well. For an important recent article about the postwar detribalization of Japan's historical time, Sebastian Conrad chose the title "What Time Is Japan?"[32] The question in Conrad's title is so good that it deserves to be applied more broadly to the three mandarinates. What time is east Asia?

The east Asian civil service examinations, like the mandarinates they created, appeared to embody, and combine, the developmental tendencies of two quite different periods in Western history. In their curricula the mandarinates' examinations had more in common with the classical education of the aristocratic preindustrial West than they did with the much more mutable civil service examinations of the contemporary West, with all their intelligence tests, aptitude tests, and psychological profiling tests.

On the other hand, the mandarinates' examinations also anticipated the civil service recruitment norms of the industrial and postindustrial West in an impressive number of ways. They enshrined public, test-based competitions for government positions, from which particularistic ties and cronyism had been rigorously excluded (even to the point of military patrols of examination sites, and of examiners being barred from knowing examinees' names, precautions that are less well developed in the contemporary West even now). They established a clear relationship between examination levels and types of government position. And they applied affirmative action to make sure that disadvantaged minorities (but not women) could participate, as in 1777, when Beijing gave the border students in China's regional examinations an amnesty period of thirty years in which to acquire the "Central Domain" speech tones necessary for understanding the poetry examinations, or as in Vietnam in the 1800s, when ethnic minorities were given privileged admission into the schools that prepared them for examinations.

Face to face with this apparent confusion in east Asian developmental time, Max Weber flinched. Or rather, he chose both to see and not to see. Writing about Confucian scholar-officials, Weber differentiated imperial China from heredity-conscious feudal Europe. He wrote that in China strangers of unknown rank would be asked how many examinations they had passed, not (as in Europe) how many ancestors of what social type they had. (At the time Weber wrote, the German world, from its high nobility to its Junker gentry, still preserved a strong feudal afterglow: in Prussia, 83 percent of the provincial prefects were nobles by birth as late as 1914, even if they had received civil service training.)[33] Yet in the same discussion, Weber bizarrely compared the impeachment of Chinese officials by Chinese government censors, not to a modern bureaucracy's surveillance of its members, but to the medieval European Catholic clergy's insistence upon the confession of sins, a more religious and less modern parallel.[34] For Weber, the mandarinates were both inside and outside modern time. They exemplified a double existence, or even—to adapt the old Ernst

Kantorowicz term—a double truth, being eternally unmodern in their essence but occasionally modern in their dispositions.

Of course the temporal perplexities go beyond the issues of civil service
examinations versus heredity. Actually, upward mobility in the three mandarinates was limited in China and Vietnam and even more limited in
Korea; at the same time, upward mobility in the more formally feudal societies of Europe was more than possible for churchmen like Wolsey or
Mazarin or Richelieu. The greater issue is the comparative development of
recognizably postfeudal forms of reasoning in defining the politically useful, and the particular powers of critical self-awareness that might accompany them. This is perhaps even more apparent in premodern east Asian
discussions of the rise of bureaucracy than in the writings of someone like
Weber, who was—in traditional east Asian terms—no more than the ex-
traordinarily gifted equivalent of a "mountain and forest scholar" who
largely stood outside the bureaucratic transactions he was exploring. As
opposed to this, the Chinese debate about meritocracy—the administrative version of the great Kantian problem of the need to make people who
are morally fallible our rulers—could be pursued, by the end of the nineteenth century, through at least twelve previous centuries' worth of critical
bureaucratic insiders' controversy about just one government institution,
the first of the six ministries, the ministry of civil appointments *(Libu)*.

What do the earliest versions of this controversy reveal? Tang dynasty
China, in the seventh century, was no more fully meritocratic than early
nineteenth-century England was democratic. Yet just as the idea of democracy was already implicated in early nineteenth-century English politics, so
too the idea of the world's "third revolution"—the rise of postfeudal professional bureaucrats—had begun to affect Chinese politics in the Tang period. In the late seventh century, in fact, a high official of the Tang ministry
of civil appointments, disturbed by the specter of rootless professionalism,
proposed that China's embryonic third revolution be halted, by neofeudal
measures such as a return to the earlier Zhou-Han system in which the
powers to select Chinese government personnel were decentralized and
distributed among high provincial authorities. The Tang official pointed
eloquently to the emerging hazards of post-aristocratic government. These
included, for him, an exaggerated dependency on one overworked ministry of personnel, rather than the entrusting of appointments to high provincial officials who personally knew the aspiring office-holders. They also
included the marketplace-like competition for positions among surplus

numbers of examination students, who could simulate virtues in the examinations' struggles without actually having them; and the shift to a reliance upon job candidates' written texts, rather than upon a more personal knowledge of their behavior, as a means of judging them.[35]

The interest of this proposal lies in the fact that, even at a time when China was largely aristocratic, its author had to frame his neofeudal appeal in a language of administrative utility. He apparently could not do so in terms of the natural virtues of inherited privileges. A major European figure like Edmund Burke, as late as the eighteenth century, could argue that broadly distributed hereditary political power of an aristocratic kind was a natural principle, whose rightness was justified by its long existence. Eleven centuries before Burke, the very basis for this quaint sort of political theory had practically vanished in China. Defenders of such a thing there had to rationalize limited refeudalizations of political power in terms that were more modern than Burke's, namely by a calculated fear of the costs of administrative expansion not moderated by forms of decentralization.

The early appearance of such a political language in east Asia points to the need for a more broadly textured history of modernity. Of course, there is an even more extreme alternative: rejection of the very notion of modernity itself as (in Georges Benko's formulation) a failed concept that actually attests an absence of concept, a term whose position as an autonomous epistemological object has never been established.[36] But as an intellectual reference point, we can probably no more avoid discussing the historical touchstones of modernity than Renaissance thinkers could avoid discussing the touchstones of the ideal commonwealth. There is a global social-class problem here as well, not just a debatable epistemological object. Few non-Western peasants, aware of the existence elsewhere of better technology and better hopes of self-advancement through education, would agree that modernity was a failed concept.

Most Asian intellectuals, at present, would undoubtedly accept the limited Eurocentrism of the "Big Ditch" theory of modernity. This theory locates the origins of much of the modern in the acceleration of the rate of scientific and technological discoveries in the West since 1600, the exponentially increasing forms in which knowledge is produced, and the awkwardnesses such a multiplication of knowledge creates for human political and social systems. Kang Youwei's eccentric sketch of the "Big Ditch" theory in the spring of 1895—Kang informed the Beijing court that the English hero Francis Bacon had saved the Western world from Papal "befuddlement" and Islamic aggression by his new doctrine of power through the increase of scientific intelligence—is an early milestone of Asian acceptance of the idea.[37] It is the difficulty of creating any structures of time that could accommodate all the other historical realms so often linked to modernity that overwhelms the narrow program of the "Big Ditch" theory of knowledge growth. What about the development of individualism—variously imputed by European historians to Europe's twelfth and thirteenth centuries, or to its sixteenth and seventeenth centuries? Or the disappearance of hereditary estates? Or the creation of political systems as acts of rational willpower not closely associated with God or religion, and the generation of forms of political criticism with a high consciousness of the artificiality and manipulability of political institutions?

In a period when the technical vocabulary for talking about global historical time in postcolonial ways is just beginning to develop, the question "What time is east Asia?" still has to be asked with reference to a Western formula that originated in Italian humanism. That formula, which divides history into "ancient," "medieval," and "modern" periods, was not even fully accepted in the West itself until the nineteenth century. Western critics of it now complain that this formula at present grips the Western academic world like a "straitjacket." It determines how we organize history departments; and the progressive, evolutionary, materialist theories of change that became popular in the West in the 1800s, as part of this formula, have somehow managed the neat trick of surviving the horrors of the twentieth century, so that their fossilized optimism continues to inform world history textbooks, albeit less confidently than before 1914. A critic like Umberto Eco would go much further: the idea of "cumulative progress," of the sort embodied in the formula, is "the great error of modern civilization."[38] The rarity of nonlinear theories in the natural and social sciences probably reflects those sciences' immaturity—not reality.

For the immediate future, however, the postcolonial study of the creative agency of non-Western societies is perhaps better served by decolonizing linear formulas of time and ending their use as tribal mechanisms of discrimination, rather than rejecting them altogether. The history of the mandarinates provides objective justification for doing so, and the psychological need is obvious: the Italian humanists would be staggered by the political hyperreality of their formula in contemporary China and Vietnam, and by the general association of ideas of time with those societies' salvation anxieties.[39]

Sebastian Conrad also shows us how postwar Japan could acquire a psychological stake in this supposedly outdated European "straitjacket" formula, using it to imagine alternative modernities. Use of the formula allowed Japanese historians to rid themselves of exceptionalist local chronologies of Japanese time, based upon the emperorship, that prewar Japanese ultranationalists had exploited to justify military expansion. The formula, by its conversion of national and regional differences into stages of time, held out the prospect that modernity was accessible to everyone; the "hermeneutic priority" of the West in the formula was thus rendered harmless.[40]

Given these possibilities, an anachronistic and Eurocentric formula of historical development can become a globally shared convention of analysis, if not a true system; like Salvador Dali's limp watches, the "straitjacket" has hidden elasticities. But if it is to be appropriated to subvert improperly narrow understandings of forms of creativity that we conventionally label "modern," there must be an acceptance that many of those forms—Athenian democracy, Roman law, the east Asian mandarinates provide examples—could develop independently of the timetables of capitalism and industrialization. The more fundamentalist uses of the "straitjacket" make it hard to appreciate that some kinds of modern political and economic reasoning did not begin with the Amsterdam stock exchange or in Enlightenment salons.

Political Hazard Analysis

One author of a recent world history, shifting the terms from economics to politics, has argued that the main story in the "world-historical process" has been a steady increase in "infrastructure" and in the "infrastructural techniques" available to power-holders and to human societies at large. Another and perhaps better world historian, more attuned to the pathos of human triumphs, has posited that the linear story is rather one of human gains in efficiency of production and social control being matched by increases in human vulnerability.[41] If the study of the modern includes the study of the expanded "conservation of catastrophe," or at least of the accumulation of hazards as well as achievements, the three east Asian mandarinates make an interesting place for examining whether the pursuit of meritocracy, however incomplete, is more or less stable, or more or less corruptible, than hereditary power is over a long period of time. Nor does this necessarily involve ignoring R. Bin Wong's wise advice to look at the common factors of the Western and east Asian political experiences rather than just their differences.[42]

One common factor involves the changing scale of political experience, and its effects. In the middle of the nineteenth century an important Chinese statecraft thinker, Wang Boxin, could see China's political history down to that point as the history of different forms of verifying human capacity, and their repercussions. He divided that history into two contrasting periods of talent validation. The first was the pre-Tang period, in which government was small in numbers, flexible in the recruitment of its officials, cautious about how officials were matched to their positions, and obsessed with the visibility of its officials' administrative experiences. The second was the period from the Tang dynasty on, when capacity and incapacity became less and less visible as government became bigger and more inclined to substitute written texts for direct experience.[43] There is a parallel here with a famous work by a European near-contemporary of Wang Boxin's, Benjamin Constant, who died in 1830. Constant saw European history as a contrast between two forms of liberty, ancient and modern. In the small ancient republics, individual political participation could be real, not abstract, even if private civil liberties had to be sacrificed to a dominant government. But in bigger, more complex modern polities, the individual, by having to be represented by others, went from an active to a fictive part in government, being compensated by a richer sphere of private happiness.

What Constant's contrast between two types of liberty and Wang's contrast between two types of meritocracy have in common is that both were concerned about the shrinking of direct political experience as political systems grew in size. Constant was anxious about the changing nature of liberty and political representation as polities expanded, an issue that lacked depth in east Asian thought. Wang was concerned about the changing nature of talent recruitment and talent measurement as polities expanded, an issue that lacked depth in Western thought. But both were using contrasting typological models to explore the transition from active to more fictive or abstract forms of political experience. The expansion of the fear of being misled, as the technical complexity of state institutions outgrew their traditional social capital, haunted both civilizations. If we cannot yet responsibly build a galactic museum of the past thousand years of world history, there is at least no need to invent some sort of galactic pidgin in order to discuss what human struggles such a museum might commemorate.

— 2 —

Meritocracy's Underworlds

No understanding of political evolution can ignore the risks or hazards that accompany various types of political change, challenging its would-be managers. Jacob Burckhardt, the Swiss historian who argued in 1860 that modernity had begun in the Italian Renaissance, with fifteenth-century Florence deserving "the name of the first modern state in the world," was careful to itemize the darker aspects of Italy's alleged modernity. The rational treatment of war, by an Italian society in which philosophy had triumphed over religion, nonetheless allowed for the worst atrocities; the ascendancy of culture over hereditary power, as in Florentine courtiers whose manner was more important than the blood in their veins, nonetheless brought with it artful forms of vengeance like the vendetta; speculation about freedom and necessity, in a context in which belief in God was no longer absolute, nonetheless was accompanied by a renewed interest in astrology and magic.[1]

Burckhardt's point was that each stage of what seemed to be progress tended to create its own characteristic underworld, as the price of its normalization. The rise of partly postfeudal mandarinates based upon managerial calculation in China, Korea, and Vietnam generated their own previously unimagined vulnerabilities. Perhaps this helps to explain the enormous popularity in all three societies of older feudal pictures of politics like those found in a text like the *Zhou li* (Rituals of Zhou). The mandarins' delight in descriptions of the ancient Zhou dynasty aristocracy was not a violation of "the rules of social development," as some modern Chinese critics have charged.[2] It was an understandable defense mechanism: a search for noncontemporaneous answers to new problems of governability among the seemingly unalienated authority figures of a bygone age. West-

38

ern historians confined to Western examples may underestimate the complexity of the consequences of the emergence of managerial polities of an incipiently postfeudal kind. And the special argument that significant risk expansion in history did not begin before capitalism is dubious on a number of counts—as a recent controversy involving an English sociologist, Anthony Giddens, and his Chinese translator and critic, Huang Ping, illustrates. As his Chinese critic sees it, Giddens's famous book *The Consequences of Modernity* (1990) presents a "monistic, Eurocentric" picture of one modernity, originating in seventeenth-century western Europe. In so doing the book defeats Giddens's own efforts to understand, not just non-European history, but even the non-European reception of the influences of European modernity itself.[3]

Giddens's argument accords a particular prominence to the question of the distribution (and the theorization) of the risks and dangers in human history. Giddens holds that there is a "disjuncture" between the premodern and the modern, characterized by the unique way in which modern institutions create risks through normatively sanctioned forms of activity, like investment markets. Behind this lies the more general assumption that the rise of capitalism—with its investment markets—is the ultimate touchstone of global change. His Chinese translator-critic will have none of it. He accuses Giddens of minimizing the historical continuity of the unbalanced distribution of risks to upper- and lower-class people; and of pretending that the leveling effect of modern science ("Chernobyl is everywhere") signifies a decline in the importance of the differences in risks among political systems, social classes, and regions.

Until very recently, the hazards of meritocracy were not a major theme in Western political thought. Immanuel Wallerstein has even claimed that capitalism in effect created meritocracy, because of capitalists' need for greater efficiency in labor power, and also because of their optimistic assumption that meritocracy could supply "mechanisms" or emollients that would soften people's resentments over capitalism's unequal economic rewards. But that assumption is mistaken, Wallerstein holds. Meritocracy is not politically stabilizing but destabilizing, yet Western thinkers have not analyzed its hazards sufficiently. Hereditary princes were "father figures"; a "yuppie is nothing but an overprivileged sibling."[4]

Wallerstein to the contrary, European thinkers did superficially address the hazards of a polity based upon the principles of meritocracy before the appearance of capitalism. Machiavelli and Pascal, to name just two, foreshadowed Wallerstein in pointing to meritocracy's potential for trouble. Pascal, in the 1600s, even commented characteristically that political power based upon merit would produce civil war, because everyone would claim to be meritorious.[5] But Pascal did not, and perhaps could not, develop this point: that had to be done in east Asia. In modern Western liberalism, to be postfeudal is to be free and equal. In east Asia, to be postfeudal (in the limited sense in which the mandarinates were) was to be insecure; and the local theorizations of these insecurities are an important if neglected part of global political thought.

The Insecurities of Textual Politics

Putting Pascal's point in more tamely sociological language, the extent to which politically ambitious people experience feelings of relative deprivation depends upon the reference groups by which they measure their positions. In societies that are even partly meritocratic, and in which noble birth no longer has a political monopoly, those reference groups are likely to be broader, and the creation of political alienation through a sense of marginalization more probable, than in circumstances where noble birth and the stratification of power are more congruent. Students who failed their civil service examinations and then rebelled against the government out of bitterness at the failure were, therefore, a highly Pascalian phenomenon. Significantly, all three mandarinates had them.

In the 1800s alone, unsuccessful students-turned-rebels included Hong Kyongnae in Korea in 1811, the Taiping Heavenly King in China in the 1840s and 1850s, and the flamboyant poet Cao Ba Quat in Vietnam in 1854. The examinations themselves provided a common classical basis for thinking of rebellion. Shared political quest myths and their risk-justifying formulas echoed across the rice fields all the way from tenth-century Korea to nineteenth-century Vietnam, put into circulation by the common examination curricula. In tenth-century Korea supporters of the founder of the Koryo kingdom invoked King Tang of the Shang and King Wu of the Zhou (the classically celebrated founders of those two ancient Chinese dynasties) as examples of righteous insurrectionists who had toppled bad governments; in northern Vietnam in 1854, Cao Ba Quat apparently mobilized his peasants with battle flags that paid homage to those same two legendary "mandate-changing" political heroes.[6]

Beyond rebellious students, the theoretically greater breadth of choice of reference groups against which to measure one's career claims stirred up fears of political instability through textual civil wars—something Pascal had not imagined. If the European discussion of the hazards of merit-based political power sometimes reflected a fear of the mob, the political analysis of this topic in the east Asian mandarinates, for many centuries, revolved around a fear of the nature of bureaucratically produced words. The treacheries of written texts in a merit-based political order were repeatedly canvassed. What subjectivities might be produced by the substitution of writing skills for hereditary social position? Or, equally problematic, by the substitution of "words" for "things," meaning practical political experience? Early modern Europe also knew a battle between "words" and "things," but the difference is revealing: it was an educational and religious battle more than a political one. (The advocates of "things" attacked pedantic grammarians for avoiding the teaching of science.) Despite the Protestant Reformation's struggle over how to interpret biblical scriptures, which gave birth to the term "hermeneutics" in the 1600s, and the important writings of philosophers like John Locke on the general uncertainties of human language, Western political theory began to acquire an equivalent specialized obsession with the illusory "transparency" of more purely legal and administrative texts only relatively recently.

Anxiety about the subjectivity of textual politics was related to anxiety about the hazards of the production of political theory itself, in a partly postfeudal world whose mediating hierarchies were weak. Alasdair MacIntyre has suggested that the claim to a special understanding of the world is characteristic of modern professional revolutionaries, of the sort found in Joseph Conrad novels or minuscule Trotskyist groups. This is because the professional revolutionaries have to base their claim to dignity and influence more upon "epistemological self-righteousness" than upon such things as hereditary wealth and social status.[7] But there is no need to look inside a Joseph Conrad novel to find such people. In east Asia many examination-system graduates, even in the less defeudalized Korea, met the description. The politics of "epistemological self-righteousness" had been embedded in the mandarinates for a long time.

There was, first of all, the effect of bureaucratic life upon political reasoning. The Chinese scholar-official Sima Guang (1019–1086) warned, in the eleventh century, that his fellow Song dynasty officials were making the "written" totally present and the "real" or the "practical" totally absent. Sima Guang attributed this tendency, and the Song bureaucracy's inability to engage in long-term planning for the public good, to the short-term appointments of its nonhereditary circulating bureaucrats. They needed quick results to get promotions. Meritocratic mobility therefore produced people who were not "careful of time" in ways that would serve the state's long-term success.[8] The public good was defined here less as a product that would emerge from the interaction of class interests than as something that would develop from the interaction of objective and subjective temporal disciplines. The criticism resembles the complaints that contemporary economists make about business corporation executives who stress immediate shareholder dividends too much.

Then there was the problem of official factionalism. Ironically, for Korean and Vietnamese thinkers as well as Chinese ones, the factionalism of the Chinese state intellectuals of the Song dynasty itself, in which Sima Guang had personally participated, came to be regarded as one of the central cautionary tales of unmediated factionalism among the self-righteous. If we just look at the east Asian debate in the 1700s about the earlier Song scholar-official factions, some critics, like Yi Ik in Korea, thought that earlier factionalism in Tang China, and above all the later factionalism of the Korean literati purges, had been worse. But Yi Ik's Vietnamese contemporary Le Quy Don, in a well-circulated text for which a Korean envoy in Beijing wrote a preface, argued that the Song court had foundered because of its mandarin elite's fondness for treating writing brushes as if they were swords, and for engaging in endless arguments that "hesitant" Song rulers could not resolve.[9] It was this general line of thought that a famous Chinese contemporary of them both, the poet and county magistrate Yuan Mei, developed as a memorable indictment of the whole text-based approach to postfeudal politics. Yuan Mei re-created the lives of the Song dynasty's "gentlemen" (junzi), as he ironically called its scholar-officials of seven hundred years earlier, as if they were some sort of dangerous historical mutation that had not been neutralized.

Yuan Mei's picture of the Song dynasty "gentlemen" (in which he specifically indicted Sima Guang, as well as numerous others) was undoubtedly licentious. But his analysis raises important comparative issues in the genealogy of the politically modern. Yuan Mei wrote that the Song dynasty had perished, not because it had too few classically educated "gentlemen" in office, but because it had too many. The Song government had been blighted not because its "gentlemen" were not public-spirited, but because they were too public-spirited, with an individual and group moral zealousness that could not be harmonized enough with that of others to permit the empire's governance. There was little reference, in Yuan Mei's essay about the Song, to the usual apparatus by which Western Sinologists habitually try to explain "traditional" Chinese politics. The emperorship itself was the most conspicuous omission. At the end of it all, Yuan Mei asked if there was any power in the Chinese state that was capable of "mediating" political disputes among masses of public-spirited officeholding "gentlemen."[10] Here, in effect, was an Asian writing-brush version of the civil war Pascal predicted, long before Pascal had predicted it.

If there ever was, from the standpoint of political history, a question that could be called modern, it would surely be Yuan Mei's: Who mediates? One scholar has recently characterized the difficulty as the "circularity of enlightened reasoning," in which the modern "self-appointed oracles" that have replaced the castes or churches of the old, pre-enlightened "agrarian polities" in telling people what to think, are themselves socially rooted but unable to validate themselves conclusively.[11] Without papal authority, or the feudal hierarchies sanctioned by European Christendom, who, or what, could mediate elite disputes about moral and political issues, and so compel rational cooperation in a complex society? After 1700, Western civilization was to try to answer the "who mediates" question with a variety of proposals, none of them entirely satisfactory. Rousseau's Legislator? Lenin's vanguard party? The invisible hand of the market? The American Supreme Court? As recently as 1695 John Locke, often regarded as one of the heralds of at least early modern thought, wrote a tract *(The Reasonableness of Christianity)* in which he still tried to answer the question by clinging to the hope that the "almighty arm" of Jesus Christ would save people from their passions. Locke wrote this even after several centuries of widespread European religious terrorism, abounding in Catholic and Protestant Osama bin Ladens. Yet Western theory could not easily break away from the notion that a miracle-working God, and God's priestly or clerical agents on Earth, could impose cooperation.

But in the Song dynasty bureaucracy, at least as Yuan Mei pictured it, the more modern situation already existed. There was no ultimate religious authority that could be invoked, and not even any congenial interpretative community of the sort Confucian literati outside the bureaucracy prized. The mediation question, in Yuan Mei's account, was provoked by too many civil philosopher officials, all of them sharing the same principles of reason-based public good, fighting over policy priorities, while claiming that all rational beings would find their proposals compelling. The closest Western analogue to this would probably be found, not in the religious schismatics of a Hobbes or a Locke, but in the competition of far more contemporary Western philosophers like the twentieth-century Americans John Rawls and Robert Nozick. Both Rawls and Nozick, inspired by social contract theory, try to imagine principles of justice that would persuade any rational actor. But they adopt different initial premises or policy priorities in doing so and then lack any rational criterion for resolving the dispute between them, there being no such criterion outside their arguments.

Yuan Mei invites us to imagine a bureaucracy with many Confucian John Rawlses and Robert Nozicks in high government positions, each with an army of disciples. At least some Korean factional warfare might also be seen in this light. Yuan Mei did not rebuke the Song emperors for not mediating the quarrels among their court officials. His unwritten assumption was that they could not do so, any more than a contemporary American president could mediate the disagreements between a John Rawls faction and a Robert Nozick faction if there were hundreds of Rawlses and Nozicks entrenched in his administration.

East Asian mandarins' suspicion of the ways writing could displace experience within a bureaucracy was just one symptom of less formally feudal power struggles. Linguistic symbols of power, as expressed in government texts, could not be privatized by any one political actor as effectively as territorial fiefs with castles, or other forms of political real estate, could be privately held by more feudal power-holders. Language, unlike feudal domains, was unstable and much more appropriable, even if Pierre Bourdieu is right to mock theories of "linguistic communism" for their suggestion that language is universally and uniformly accessible, regardless of social circumstances.[12]

In all three mandarinates an awe of verbal power concealed the insecurity involved in its bureaucratic uses. In east Asia the king's body was not thought to be divided into public and private capacities, as in European thought going back to Cicero; the monarchy was idealized as a verbal force that the ruler shared with his mandarins, who claimed to be the king's "throat and tongue." In parts of medieval and early modern Europe the king's touch was supposed to cure sick people. In eastern Asia it was the king's words (or words addressed to the king by his mandarins) that were thought to be therapeutic. As his inspector general informed an early Choson Korean king, it was his minister's duty to offer words of remonstrance that would cure his ailments. Statecraft thinkers in China wrote essays on "the words of the king" which compared such words to the light of the sun or the noise of thunder, provided the king had the right mandarin speechwriters and expositors. The Han emperors' proclamations, later Chinese rulers were told, had been moving enough to attract diseased and aged people, who postponed their wish to die after listening to them.[13]

One unique institution in this texts-dominated political culture concentrated east Asian governments' ambivalence about the literary practices of their own officials. The same term "office of censors" (*Yushidai* in Chinese; *Osadae* in Korean; *Ngu su dai* in Vietnamese) was in use in China from the Later Han to the Ming, in Korea from the tenth to the fourteenth centuries (when it changed into the famous "Three Offices" or *Samsa*), and in Vietnam from the thirteenth to the eighteenth centuries. The term referred originally to the royal scribes of the Zhou period. With the bureaucracy and its examinations, the ancient royal scribes turned into something quite different and distinctive to mandarinates: censors, licensed inside critics, symbols of the bureaucracy's need to reflect upon its own behavior. The censors operated as a text-based, rather than a birthright-based, antidote to false forms of mediation.

Among historians of the British empire in India, there has been a debate about the effectiveness of the British colonial rulers' control of their own administrative language as they used it to invade, and redefine, the "epistemological spaces" of Indian society. Some scholars have argued that the British colonizers were able to impose their own political language on their Indian subalterns; others have suggested that the subordinate arenas of information production of the Indians themselves could transform from below, and undermine, the linguistic strategies of British domination.[14] But British India was a colonial police state. It had coercive powers of mediation, externally based, such as none of the east Asian mandarinates possessed. It surely offers a narrower spectacle of the potential contestations of administrative language within a political system than the mandarinates, where the mediation problem made the debate more acute.

The mediation issue, connected to conflicts over definitions of merit, was so sensitive that administrative language could be contested from below by subaltern officials' silence, not just by their participation. If the "words officials," as the censors were known, made a tactical withdrawal from the language games within the government, that could distort the games' outcomes as much as their aggressive involvement could. One Vietnamese ruler, in 1456, explicitly recognized the dangers of his censors' withdrawals: he warned them not to "close their mouths" and remain mute. But if the "words officials" could not remain voiceless, strong rulers had an incentive to keep them as historyless as possible and deny them the means to systematize their agency's own norms of linguistic intervention. In China the emperor, in 1774, vigorously beat back a proposal by censors to compile "case precedents" *(zeli)* for their agency comparable to the codified case precedents of the government's six ministries. Language itself might seem perilously difficult to control; rulers could at least block the development of an institutional memory of how court officials had tried to appropriate it.

In Korea, where kings were weak, it was another matter. Critics of the Korean censoring organs like Yu Suwon (1694–1755) saw that the argumentative young men based in them, although political subalterns in theory, had more or less captured the Korean government from below. Their literary skill, their aptitude for collecting opinions, and their collusion with other officials, had been their weapons. Yu Suwon characterized the violence of the youthful power-hungry Korean government censors of the 1700s in language that journalists today might well use to describe the ringleaders of a soccer riot.[15] The cause of the problem was a bureaucratic state without sufficient authority to decide who was meritorious and deserving of promotion and who was not. Pascal's proposition—that meritocracy would threaten civil strife because all members of a meritocratic elite would acquire an absolute belief in their own merit—was vindicated in Korea long before it could be tested in Europe.

Elite Self-Esteem Tensions

Fears about the subjectivity of official language were matched by fears about the increased subjectivity of status evaluations in a post-aristocratic society. Mandarins' self-esteem was not, as in aristocratic societies, largely a reflex of the honor due to them by virtue of their positions in a fixed social order. It was also, in some instances primarily, a product of their success at the examination sites and in the government administration. But the mass society of the examinations, and the shallowness of many of the examinations' forms, often seemed to make the self-esteem they created illusory. As one of many Chinese critics put it, the criterion of success through written tests had led to an academicization of the ideal of "capacity" such that the officials who triumphed in these tests were really lifeless copies of the ideal of the "person of talent" (Chinese: *rencai;* Korean: *inchae;* Vietnamese: *nhan tai*), not genuine embodiments of it. They were like motionless statues of racehorses that could suggest the horse's physique but not its speed; or like wooden carvings of wild geese that could simulate the bird's wings and feathers but not its flight dynamics.[16]

The east Asian mandarinates' pioneering invention of standardized methods of identifying "capacity," on a nonhereditary basis, therefore led to a major form of hazard analysis in their political theory. During and after World War Two, when batteries of psychological tests and ratings scales were first applied to Western army soldiers, the same doubts began to emerge in Western thought. Western psychologists discovered that something like the IQ test oversimplified the problem of human capacity; earlier psychologists had wrongly concluded that IQ tests and learning capacity were synonymous. But in preindustrial east Asia this was already old news. Such stilted examination forms as the famous eight-legged essay had had something of the same fetishistic functions in the measurement of human ability there, once heredity-based assumptions about it had waned, as the IQ test has had much more recently in the West.

Analysis of the inadequacies of elite self-esteem and its dangers inevitably led, in the mandarinates, to the problem of corruption in office. In his general reform memorial to the Song emperor in the eleventh century, Wang Anshi had focused upon the link between official corruption and low salaries. Wang argued that it was a first principle of politics that officials' "modesty and sense of shame" had to be "nourished" by salary increases. There was nothing here about there being an elite self-esteem that reflected an inner satisfaction at successfully embodying heroic or aristocratic values, Confucian or otherwise. Status ethics here were assumed to be conditioned from without, through government techniques of encouragement. Most Chinese officials, Wang wrote, were inevitably moral chameleons, or "middling people," who would behave like "gentlemen" if they had decent salaries, but like "petty people" if their pay was poor; only a minority were either innately "gentlemen" (incorruptible although poor) or innately "petty" (behaving corruptly even if well paid.)[17]

Writing on the same subject six hundred years later, another would-be Chinese reformer, Gu Yanwu, did not even bother to divide officials into three different moral types as Wang had, thereby minimizing still further the importance of their inner moral identities. The key to fighting corrup-

tion, Gu maintained, was to enable officials to "know their own importance" through decent government stipends. Unfortunately, Chinese officialdom had been gradually impoverished over the centuries, through
the acceleration of their defeudalization. Old-fashioned payments to government officials in crops and rents, derived from appanage lands they
had been granted, had been replaced by centrally paid money salaries, to
the point that seventeenth-century Chinese government officials' income
amounted to only a third or less (Gu thought) of what bureaucrats had effectively earned centuries earlier in the Tang dynasty.[18]

Thinkers like Wang and Gu could quite plausibly, if rather grandly, be
seen as two of the world's earliest theoreticians of postfeudal elite insecurity. They were addressing the question of how to create a plunder-proof
elite with a publicly dedicated service ethic, rather than merely disguised
self-aggrandizing instincts, in a society whose rulers were as much made as
born. This was a modern question, even if their answers were not; some industrial countries today, with greater assets than preindustrial east Asia,
have still to solve it. A consciousness of the fragility of the sense of purpose, the teleology, upon which any postfeudal public service ethic had to
be based was built into the command systems of the mandarinates. This
gave their debates about corruption a tragic dimension that the more common Western explanations of the phenomenon (such as the illicit penetra-
tion of the government by private interests, or the illicit marketization of
government assets to rent-seeking privateers) do not often capture. Even
now, because of the longer survival of a more fully aristocratic political
power in Europe, the Western analysis of the political consequences of the
loss of self-esteem within ruling classes seems thin by east Asian standards.
The greater preference in the West still appears to be to analyze the loss of
self-esteem within aboriginal populations or racial minorities.

Yet it must be added that in the two smaller mandarinates, where more
feudal principles of politics remained more accessible and older forms of
rewards for official stewardship survived, the issue mattered less. In a reversal of the Chinese pattern, money salaries for Vietnamese officials were
replaced, between 1500 and 1800, by court grants of revenue-producing
appanage lands, in the south (Cochinchina) even by the assignment to
them of menial laborers (a practice more familiar in Southeast Asia than in
China). Northern Vietnamese rulers in the 1700s acknowledged this partial refeudalization of their political life by taking a Chinese government
salary formula called "nourishment of virtue" cash payments and converting it into appanage lands for Vietnamese officials known as "nourishment

of virtue fields." Korea remained closer to China in form by phasing out its office lands and rank lands, in favor of an official salary system, by the late 1500s. But by that time the *yangban* elite had become a landholding quasi-aristocracy, much more secure than Gu Yanwu's poor scholar-officials. Korean envoys to China in the 1700s were important witnesses to China's bureaucratic corruption; their shocked reports about it suggest that it was greater than anything they knew at home.[19]

Apart from increased salaries, another external remedy for the insufficiency of the mandarins' self-esteem—connected as it was to their epistemological self-righteousness—was the state's rationing of non-economic status perquisites in the mandarins' favor. But this inflamed the "upstairs downstairs" question found in all meritocracies. (In contemporary universities, for example, it is embodied in the division between tenured professors and sessional lecturers.) Just how far down was the post-aristocratic, meritocratic order to be projected, in social and administrative terms? All three mandarinates were governed not just by bureaucrats but by "sub-official functionaries," a term that went back to the Tang (Chinese: *xuli*; Korean: *sori*; Vietnamese: *tu lai*). They were the clerks who performed the more menial tasks in government offices, and they lacked civil service rank. Were they to be part of the post-aristocratic political culture? Or were they to be condemned to be the representatives of a "primordial" cronyism, based upon hereditary corporatism rather than merit, who parasitically colonized the government from below?

Outside the monarchy, one Chinese scholar-official noted in the middle of the 1800s, the defeudalization principle had succeeded everywhere in eliminating hereditary power, except in two places: the ethnic minority chiefs of China's southwest, and the clerks and servants in government offices. The clerks' hereditary claims to their lowly positions had not been challenged. Some clerks and servants could have a high opinion of their lineages, such as the clerks in one Beijing government office who claimed to be the descendants of honorable families of the late Ming dynasty (1368–1644). But in both the capital city and the provinces all the clerks were entrenched, taking advantage of the fact that they were permanent and the officials above them were subject to bureaucratic appointment and transfer cycles. The problem of the hereditary clerks was an irresolvable one, the scholar-official thought. Perhaps it was the only truly irresolvable problem in the Chinese government; other problems, such as the regional warlordism that had been common to feudalism, were more manageable.[20]

Irresolvable or not, the postfeudal "revenge of the clerks" was a crisis with a modern flavor. It was anticipated in Europe on the eve of the French Revolution by the critics of postfeudal mass education (such as Voltaire) who warned that the end of hierarchical obligations would induce everyone to want to be a tonsured cleric rather than a manual worker. How would manual workers behave when they could not be tonsured clerics? Marginalization under a "careers open to talent" mandarinate, in which human worth rested upon seemingly subjective perceptions of merit rather than upon birth, was more provocative than marginalization under a strong feudal hierarchy. It produced political pathologies of a type that east Asia had to face before Europe. Indeed it could be hypothesized that "cronyism" among the clerks, far from being an eternal "Confucian" reflex, was actively produced by precocious preindustrial bureaucracies that needed such insulating mechanisms to soften the transition from politics based on feudal hierarchies to a politics based upon administrative utility.

The debate about the clerks spanned east Asia. Characteristically, thinkers in the two smaller mandarinates seem to have preferred neofeudal remedies. Equally typically, Korean neofeudal remedies involved genealogical issues and Vietnamese ones did not. One Korean writer, in a history of the "clerkly" stratum published in 1848, asserted that rural sub-officials *(hyangni)* had once had the same bloodlines as the *yangban* class; they therefore ought to be treated as *yangban*. Only in Korea could the extension of caste-based ideals be applied as a partial solution for the resentments of people marginalized in a government machine based upon promotion by merit. In Vietnam, where the problem of clerks emerged later than in China or Korea, Phan Huy Chu in the early 1800s revived the feudal temptation in a different way. Pointing to the extended princely households in the *Zhou li* (Rituals of Zhou), in which literati had allegedly done all the clerical work and there had been no clerks, he proposed a purge in which Confucian scholars should simply reclaim from the clerks all the Vietnamese government's clerical functions, allowing the despised clerks to disappear.

China's size prevented any realistic neofeudal remedies comparable to the ones proposed by Korean and Vietnamese thinkers. So the remedies proposed in China tended to be more postfeudal, namely extending the examinations to at least some clerks as well. A Chinese political giant, the eighteenth-century Grand Secretary Chen Hongmou, correctly and courageously pointed out that the clerks were the victims of a meritocratic elitism that had failed to develop fully. Far from being an incurable pathology, the clerks were the unfinished business of Chinese history. The examination system, when it grew, had failed to incorporate the clerks because the architects of the original seventh-century examinations had been unduly influenced by the eccentric patterns of aristocratic partitioning peculiar to the period when China had been divided, before the Tang dynasty. The delayed effect of these patterns had induced the Chinese state to think of the clerks as being uneducable and outside the pale. Radically revising the clerks' negative identity, Chen Hongmou demanded that the process for examinations and promotions be offered to some of them too (it was not); they shared, with mandarins, a natural goodness and inclination to self-improvement.[21]

But extending the examinations to the clerks would have diluted the distinction of being a mandarin. This distinction was more precarious (as the theoretical concern with salaries indicated) than that of a hereditary aristocrat. Extending the examinations might also have flooded the labor market for official appointments. Unlike industrial Western countries, whose warfare and growing capacity to concentrate surplus capital encouraged them to increase their bureaucracies' size (once they became fully bureaucratic), eighteenth-century China was not expanding its formal officialdom. The emperor of China whom Chen Hongmou served complained that he had to "meditate in the middle of the night" about how merely to "dredge" the blockages in the existing appointments system that kept regional examination winners waiting for thirty years or more for suitable government jobs.[22]

Other Chinese reformers saw the clerks problem as one caused by the worsening inverse relationship between the rank of bureaucrats and the degree of their direct social engagement, as everybody tried to move to the top of the hierarchy. Higher officials devoted more attention to controlling lower officials than to addressing local needs. Lower officials, under pressure from their superiors, were overworked and relied all the more upon their more locally knowledgeable clerks, who were not subject to bureaucratic transfers. That meant having to indulge the interests of their clerks. The result was a Chinese anticipation, centuries before European sociologists discovered the phenomenon, of what would now be called goal displacement: the substitution, within the government, of the government's professed goals by other priorities that often undermined them.[23]

The implications of the east Asian debate about clerks for global history have yet to be appreciated. Is there a linear trend in preindustrial world history toward the "one-directional" expansion of power by political systems, through a steady increase in the infrastructure available to "power-holders," as Michael Mann claims? Or is it true that for every gain in coordinated power in human history there have been accompanying increases in vulnerability to breakdown, as William McNeill suggests?[24] The east Asian experiment with bureaucracy upholds the second view. Goal displacement, or the bureaucratic introversion of agency, as the number of officials who managed other officials increased and lesser officials allied themselves with clerks in response, served to make the very notion of political agency itself uncertain. Anxiety about this hazard had deeper roots in preindustrial eastern Asian political theory than in its Western equivalent.

Postfeudal Loyalty Concerns

Chen Hongmou's plea for a more comprehensive mandarinization of Chinese politics shows how the ideal of "people of talent" could transcend the everyday limits of class (and ethnic) prejudice, despite the hazards of the ideal so well known to so many critics. There was one more hazard that it is perhaps easier to infer than to document. That was the inadequate capacity of a mandarinate, compared with political systems based upon a feudal service ethic or mass nationalism, to mobilize large numbers of people for goals they could not immediately identify as their own. Popular commitment to the merit-rewarding institutions, as expressed in the pursuit of "honor" and "fame" through success in examinations, was not the same thing as a more general political obligation relying upon forms of loyalty that could be readily emotionalized.

Confucian philosophers, of course, asserted that the totalization of one virtue, filial piety, would solve the problem. From the exhaustive development of filial piety would surely spring loyalty to the ruler, respect for elders, trustworthiness in friends, an end to political calamities, and the disappearance of rebellions (as one seventeenth-century Chinese official, Tang Bin, hopefully argued). But arguments like these maximized filial piety to such a degree that it became weightlessly utopian. They also failed to conceal the fact that political loyalty, even in this utopian mode, was at best a secondary reflex.

It is difficult to answer the question, even with polltakers, of how much the various people in any society genuinely internalize the norms, values, and beliefs that legitimize its social order—as opposed to offering a practical compliance with them. So it is necessary to be cautious. All three mandarinates certainly produced mandarins who were willing to lay down their lives for the dynasties that had employed them. But the mandarinates also produced educational treatises that warned about unscrupulous "cleverness" in children as they began to pursue examination success. Some of these treatises even went so far as to suggest that "dull" people were less of a threat to the administrative world than more selfish knowledgeable and talented ones.[25]

In China, where the question of political obligation in an individualistic examination-system culture was hugely magnified by the scale of the polity, important eighteenth-century scholar-officials warned the court to preserve the remaining hereditary power of the southwest ethnic minority leaders, rather than destroy it. To such officials this was the key to the simple obedience of the minority militia soldiers who were necessary to the defense of the empire's frontiers.[26]

An interest in the selective preservation of old feudal ties in parts of China was matched by efforts to create new symbols of loyalty elsewhere. There were, for example, the women who were honored for martyring themselves, through suicide, to avoid second marriages that might compromise their fidelity to dead first husbands. Such extreme behavior was morally problematic on a number of counts. Yet female fidelity (a woman should not have two husbands) and male political loyalty (a minister should not serve two rulers) were thought to correspond to each other. And the spectacular proliferation of curious stone monuments to female fidelity in Qing China suggests that the cult of female fidelity was being used, in part, as a catalyst for encouraging the attempted regeneration of male political obligation. Indeed some Chinese writers in the 1800s specifically compared female suicides committed out of loyalty to dead first husbands to the service-to-the-death pledges (weizhi) made by ministers to their princes thousands of years earlier in the prebureaucratic feudal period.[27] In the mandarinates the memory of this ancient feudal ceremony of servants volunteering their own self-extinction to their princes served as an uncomfortable reminder of the relative decline of male political loyalty after the introduction of merit-based examinations. Susan Mann has usefully observed that Chinese discourse about marriage before 1911 was "a metonymic comment on larger social issues of mobility and class."[28] But it was also a metonymic comment on politics. The female fidelity shrines of

the Chinese mandarinate resemble nothing so much as the public ceno-
taphs to dead soldiers of World War One in the Western world after 1918.
They had the same aura of moral distinctiveness conferred on the families
of the martyred dead, whether Western soldiers or Qing Chinese women;
and the same implied moral questioning of living survivors whose spirit of
sacrifice for a seemingly greater good had never been so conclusively put to
the test.

Anxieties about the defeudalization of loyalty, however limited, finally
came to a head in the mandarinates, especially in China, in the face of
Western imperialism. Japan, the one east Asian country that had not been
a mandarinate or recruited its officials through examinations, became an
ideal reference point for reformers for many reasons; but the lure of its still
feudal national cohesiveness must surely have been one of them. Japanese
bystanders (such as Ogyü Sorai, 1666–1728) had warned that bureaucratic
polities based upon examinations sanctioned selfishness along with upward mobility. By 1906 Qing government reformers were prepared to see
in the then—prime minister of Japan, Prince Saionji, the perfect antidote
to the postfeudal inconsistencies of status that plagued the mandarinates:
Saionji fused social nobility (as a hereditary court noble) with educational
training (a decade of study in Europe) with political power (as prime minister). All "constitutional countries" that constructed themselves from the
top down, one reformer in China wrote, needed self-confident hereditary
elites whose members would owe strong obligations of loyalty and *no-
blesse oblige* to the countries they served. The reformer then proposed that
China, in effect, renounce the whole direction of the past ten centuries of
its history by creating a Japanese-style House of Peers *(Kizakuin)* and
Peers' College *(Gakushüin)* in Beijing. The object would be to quickly
manufacture hundreds of Chinese and Manchu Prince Saionjis, who could
save China by more completely reuniting political power with high, fixed
social status.[29] But it was too late. When the dying Qing court did experiment with a Japanese-style Peers' College, it was, as the old joke goes, like
an American character in an English movie: not very convincing. Fantasies
aside, there was no real hereditary nobility in China; so the College had to
admit the sons of degree-holding senior officials, lengthening the shadow
of the mandarinate as it did so.

A century later, it is possible to see the mandarins and the experiment
they reflected in more detached terms. For centuries, the mandarinates
dedicated themselves, however falteringly, to a form of political rational-

ity—the consolidation of the supremacy of scholars' knowledge over aristocrats' hereditary statuses—that remained no more than a daydream for a long line of Western thinkers from Plato to Thomas More.[30] Their critical power—their capacity to give themselves accounts of what they could and could not achieve—was itself part of the experiment. So was the magnetism of the ideal of the formally classless "person of talent." The full potentialities of the ideal—as in Huang Zongxi's hope in the 1600s that Chinese schools could be used to do everything from controlling emperors to improving mortality rates, or as in Ortai's ambition in the 1700s to create "people of talent plans" for backward Chinese provinces—were never realized. But the ideal's persuasiveness remained intact, despite all its acknowledged hazards.

As for hereditary monarchs, who stood in such an ambiguous position to the experiment, it is possible that the need for the monarchy, far from reflecting insufficient social change, grew stronger in direct proportion to the meritocracy's insecurities. The Vietnamese rebel who made himself emperor of Vietnam between 1788 and 1792 announced that he was doing so because there was a popular desire for a simple and socially humble person like himself to "help the world."[31] This was a different, more mythic way of reducing complexity and contingency from the bureaucracy's way of doing it, with examinations and time deadlines and manipulable texts. The hazards of political evolution gave the mandarinates a split personality such as our simpler theoretical timetables of what is modern cannot accommodate. The growth of bureaucratic rationality and the continuing wish for personalized forms of transcendence in politics probably fed off each other. An irony like that would surely have been appreciated by Jacob Burckhardt.

— 3 —

Administrative Welfare Dreams

Despite the mandarinates' clerks problem, and the hazards of goal displacement within their administrations that the clerks partly embodied, the professed goals of the mandarinates—and the family resemblances of the means and institutions used to achieve them—deserve scrutiny. R. Bin Wong rightly sees them as at least partly foreshadowing the welfare bureaucracies that the West came to know in the twentieth century. Imperial China's state-sponsored granaries for famine relief, according to Wong, "represented official commitments to material welfare beyond anything imaginable, let alone achieved, in Europe . . . To think of state concerns for popular welfare as a very recent political practice makes sense only if we again limit ourselves to Western examples."[1]

The two smaller mandarinates of Korea and Vietnam attempted modest versions of China's managerial welfare strategies. They even appear to have shared the same cycles of court planning to put them into effect. At the end of the 1300s the rulers of both Korea and Vietnam experimented with similar programs of equalizing land reform laws, King Taejo (Yi Songgye) of Korea in 1390 and Ho Quy Ly of Vietnam in 1397. In the 1860s both the Taewongun in Korea and the emperor Tu-duc in Vietnam tried to remedy the weaknesses of their governments by enforcing, or renewing, similar systems of village granaries that could protect against food shortages.

For many, the very notion of a welfare state is surely unimaginable without the fiscal resources, professional services, and negotiating networks of capitalism. Again we confront the question: How absolute a divide in human history did the emergence of capitalism create, in attitudes (such as the desire to use political power to strengthen social ethics) as well as in methods? Some differences are obvious. In the mandarinates the classical welfare strategies of Confucian thinkers had originated in an age when grain and cloth were the media of exchange; they assumed the primacy of agriculture and were suspicious of private property. All this made them harder to enforce and even seriously to imagine in circumstances of commercial growth. Modern welfare strategies are far more flexible in their interactions with capitalism. But echoes of the present are possible to discern in the hazards the mandarinates encountered with their administratively produced forms of agency, less mediated as they were by feudal hierarchies (at least in China and Vietnam) than in preindustrial Europe. The longer east Asian experience with at least embryonic forms of managerial politics shows how attempted extensions of elite bureaucratic rationality over the centuries could encourage their own reversal, even their own disguised refeudalization, as they became detached from local needs. Contemporary welfare states, with their far more highly developed state machinery and sense of citizenship and their greater variety of economic assets, may not know the same limits to their capacity for rational intervention. But east Asian history offers some not wholly irrelevant cautionary tales, if we dispense with fundamentalist views of modern time as totally "disjunctured."

All three mandarinates harbored a tension between smaller, more realistic views of the government's tasks and larger, more salvationist views of them. The tension expressed itself in a curious kind of political theory that combined empirical realism and normative idealism, rather than separating them. It has been said that European political thought for many centuries, with its thousands of "mirrors for the prince" texts and their catalogues of the virtues, was principally concerned with how a society ought to be governed, almost neglecting the empirical study of how societies actually were governed.[2] The actively serving bureaucrats who produced so much of the mandarinates' political theory were more likely to blend the two concerns. Their mixture of prophetic and administrative vocabularies even has a parallel in the way some contemporary social scientists struggle to distinguish their prescriptive ambitions from their analytical functions, confusing the roles of social engineers and scientists. Such east Asian statecraft formulas as "manage the state and help the age" (an abbreviation of which serves as the contemporary word for "economy" in Chinese, Korean, and Vietnamese: *jingji, kyongje, kinh te* respectively) summarized the fusion of bureaucratic utility considerations with dreams of improved popular welfare. So did such things as the title of Korea's great seventeenth-century tax reform, the *Taedongbop* (Great Uniformity Law), which took its name from the utopia in the ancient classic the *Liji* (Record of Rituals) and was administered by a government office called the Agency to Bestow Blessings *(Sonhyech'ong).*[3] Something called a golden age tax could hardly have been plausible outside a mandarinate.

The Prominence of Ancient Welfare Ideals

The adventures of one particular and persistent project of attempted social engineering in the three mandarinates, which can only be sketched here, probably best demonstrate the east Asian symbiosis of social salvation aims with administrative calculation. This was the "equal fields" system, actually practiced in parts of China from the fifth to the eighth centuries. Its proponents wanted to recapture the spirit of the supposed welfare ideals of the ancient "three dynasties" (Chinese: *san dai;* Korean: *sam dae;* Vietnamese: *tam dai*—the Xia, Shang, and Zhou dynasties before the Chinese empire). The "equal fields" system was perhaps east Asia's single most famous "compromising" adaptation (to quote James Palais) of the even more far-reaching system of public ownership and landholding equality, known as the "well-field" model, that had supposedly existed under the three dynasties. In turn this myth of the humanitarian creativity of these three feudal dynasties, widespread in all the mandarinates, became a curious backward-looking projection of a faith in the creative power of post-feudal administrators themselves.

The "equal-fields" system had combined the administrative ambition to create greater numbers of landowning, and therefore taxpaying, farmers with the salvationist aim of restraining the land aggrandizements of the rich and reducing poverty. The real-life version of the system had declined in China by the Tang dynasty. But as a dream, if not much more, it remained an intrinsic part of the elite "three dynasties" consciousness of Korean and Vietnamese scholar-officials as well as of many Chinese ones. At the end of the 1300s Korea attempted a major land reform; the language of one of the Korean government's most important advisers, Chong Tojon (d. 1398), in his essay on the land question, was almost interchangeable with the language used by Li Anshi (443–493), the bureaucratic proponent of the first "equal fields" system, in Northern Wei dynasty China, some nine centuries earlier. The last effort by an east Asian mandarinate to impose an "equal fields" system from above occurred in Vietnam's Binh Dinh province in 1839—about fourteen hundred years after this special form of conditional bureaucratic utopia had been invented in north China.[4]

Bureaucratic interpreters of the "equal fields" tradition assumed that poverty was politically created, rather than being eternal or inevitable. Their view that the poor might be no more than political or administrative by-products can be traced back to classical texts like Mencius, written in a feudal society in which hereditary power was a commonplace. In a great irony, this ancient text became more important as Chinese and other east Asian societies became progressively less like the society in which it had been written.

Anti-Mencian thinkers, who were a not-insignificant minority, might accuse the text of promoting a disastrously simple (and internally inconsistent) view of human nature, or of indulging in a vague, sentimental political subjectivism. The text nonetheless provided bureaucrats with a general theory of the social good that prevented their policy debates from degenerating into an exclusive preoccupation with administrative techniques and irrelevant turf battles. Moreover, mandarins were less constrained by feudal statuses and ancient privileges than the rulers in the text itself had been; they could treat material entitlements more freely as contingent categories; in this way the Mencian view of the poor gained an unforeseen strength in their minds as the view itself aged. Against the long-continuing eastern Asian belief that bad politics created poverty, Europeans were predisposed for many centuries to think of the poor as contemptible idlers; or (in mercantilist thought) as economic traitors to the national economy; or as vehicles of spiritual redemption for alms-giving rich people; or even as Christ's representatives on earth, as in Pierre deBlois's medieval characterization of the poor person as *vicarius Christi*.[5]

Texts like Mencius were also tested in the civil service examinations. The examinations, in this and other respects, undoubtedly contributed to the formation of a political culture in which poverty was regarded as a political symptom, and therefore as an administrative issue. All major preindustrial civilizations probably harbored a crisis in the relationship between their artificial school world, dedicated as it was to the ideals of a revered classical antiquity, and the mundane world of careers beyond the schools. In both European and east Asian preindustrial schools, in Anthony Grafton's words, "we see the ancients made to live again as political counsellors."[6] Political education was classical history, in which ancient institutions were glorified.

But thanks to the examinations, the separation between the school world and the world beyond the school was not as extreme in the east Asian mandarinates as it was elsewhere. In Europe classical history supplied models of alienated or disestablished virtues with sometimes revolutionary potentialities: ancient Roman republican figures raised awkward questions about the legitimacy of European royal absolutisms. (Thomas Hobbes, in the 1600s, went so far as to blame universities for the English revolution, because they furnished young Englishmen "with arguments for liberty out of the works of Aristotle, Plato, Cicero, Seneca, and out of the histories of Rome and Greece.")[7] The east Asian examinations, by creating a more direct relationship than the European one between worldly success and the classics taught in the schools, softened the contradictions between the pedagogical world and the bureaucratic one. The result was to stimulate, not the desire for revolution from outside the government, but the urge to legislate at least limited welfare-expansion formulas from inside it.

But as the mandarinates' societies became more complex, the odds against the success of such urges lengthened, in ways that seem partly reminiscent of theories of the decomposition of state power in industrialized societies. Reinterpreted over the centuries, "three dynasties" visions, like constitutional ones, harbored a mixture of meanings that—as Yuan Mei implied—needed more mediation than they were likely to get. In the conversion of political problems into administrative ones, the elite pursuit of administrative goals threatened to become an end in itself. In the long run this might lead not to greater welfare but to the hazard of forms of public apathy that were as dangerous in their own way as the violent activisms that European political and religious struggles generated.

Government tax policies, in particular, were part of the mandarinates' pursuit of greater human welfare, as they are in contemporary welfare states. And struggles over tax policies played a part in the conversion of political problems (like poverty) into administrative concerns in which the representation of popular needs weakened, and the welfare of individual taxpayers became blurred or displaced.

Bureaucratic Tax Reforms on Trial

Like income entitlements, tax rates could be treated by the mandarinates as contingent categories, subject to change from above, in societies that, unlike much of Europe before 1789, did not have provinces, nobles, or clergy with supposedly fixed and immutable feudal tax immunities and other privileges. (Informal tax evasions, for example by the *yangban* elite in Korea, were another matter.) Even in Vietnam, the mandarinate whose bureaucratic centralization was least secure and whose historical records were least well preserved, a major figure like Phan Huy Chu, writing in the early 1800s, could try to trace the genealogy of a Vietnamese national tax system back to the year 1013. Had Hegel been Korean or Vietnamese rather than German, he might very well have made the history of taxes a major element in his scheme of human evolution.

Classical tax policy doctrine, going back to such texts as Mencius, urged not merely that bad government produced poverty, but that an ideal low standardized tax rate—of no more than ten percent of the harvest or of general income—was the basis of mass welfare and thus of good government. The faith in the benefits of the ancient ten percent tax rate belonged to the more salvationist side of the east Asian mandarin ideal. Or at least it belonged to an exaggerated belief in the welfare functions of taxes, what the tough-minded Chinese critic Wang Fuzhi (1619–1692) condemned as the overweening "ten thousand capabilities" *(wan neng)* view of taxes.[8] Salvationist tax formulas came under varying degrees of pressure in China, Vietnam, and Korea, perhaps in direct relation to the expansion of those societies' money economies and the growth in complexity of their administrative tasks.

In China, the belief in the absolute ten percent standard for fair taxes collapsed by the Tang and Song dynasties. Thinkers of that period like Ye Shi (1150–1223), rejecting Mencius, proposed that the legitimacy of a taxation rate was determined by changing circumstances, not by an eternally unchanging ideal. For a civilization that believed that poverty and administrative practices were connected, this suggestion was like justifying the abandonment of a fourteen-centuries-old moral gold standard. But the claim that fair tax rates should fluctuate according to the degree of service, or competence, of the government, raised managerial issues at the expense of salvationist ones. It also ran the risk that theoretical debates about taxes might become increasingly self-referential, among the bureaucrats themselves, and estranged from social realities. Which manager would decide what the tax rate should be?

The most important such manager in east Asian history was probably the Tang dynasty tax reformer Yang Yan (727–781), the author of China's famous "two taxes" law of 780 c.e. This law was a watershed in world history. The "two taxes" reform replaced the old three-part land-labor-household *(zuyongtiao)* tax, which had targeted individual male taxpayers, and as such had been associated with the "equal fields" system that had been

implemented in north China three centuries earlier. Its disappearance implied that the old dream of a legislated end to agrarian inequalities would
be an implicit casualty of this eighth-century tax reform. Yang Yan's consolidation of all taxes into two simple payments, in the summer and the
fall, was an elite planner's intoxication; but it shifted the tax collectors' focus away from people to property acreages, depersonalizing ties between
the state and its subjects in its effort at fiscal rationalization.

What Yang Yan's administrative revolution showed was that, by the
eighth century, Chinese elites possessed what they thought was an untram-
meled capacity to impose massive consolidating tax reforms from the top
down; a capacity that few of Europe's much smaller governments would
have considered possible before the French Revolution, given the continued existence of feudal barriers to such actions. Even in the most tightly
organized European states in the 1700s, like Frederick the Great's Prussia,
the king did not dare to abolish the immunity from taxes that so many of
his nobles enjoyed; Frederick had to fight his many wars with revenues
from directly owned crown domains, plus British subsidies.[9]

No Western historian who has seriously examined Yang Yan's tax reforms has ever doubted their importance for histories of world development. In a 1992 collection of essays about "the global condition" William
McNeill suggested that the reforms were a landmark factor in China's pioneering shift from a command economy to a market-directed one. When
Yang Yan permitted the conversion of taxes from kind to money payment,
he legitimized the significant enlargement of market behavior in Chinese
society. This prepared the way for the more general "onset of modern
times," which McNeill locates in the China that emerged within three centuries of Yang Yan's legislation.

In effect McNeill adopted one side of a contentious Chinese debate
about China's eighth-century tax reforms, a debate that can probably be
traced back to pioneering historians of Chinese fiscal administration of the
postimperial era like Hu Jun in the 1920s. Other Chinese historians since
then have complained that Yang Yan's switch to money taxes repeatedly
lapsed in succeeding centuries; that there were acute regional differences in
Chinese tax collections; and that earlier tax-collecting habits that reformers like Yang Yan had sought to abolish recurred.[10]

But here the concern is with Yang Yan's tax reform, and its consequences, purely in terms of the precocious dynamic of bureaucratic rationalization and its pitfalls in a preindustrial empire eleven centuries before

Max Weber. Anticipating modern bureaucracies, Chinese officials produced new problems in the effort to solve old ones. The new problems were then incorporated into representations of the state as solutions to old difficulties. And Chinese officials' awareness that the real world would never completely coincide with such rationalizations, given the tendency of administrative planning to produce unintended results, also had a modern flavor. The unintended results were an ironic (or despairing) reminder of the limits of their applied human reason.

As one example, a conscientious Qing dynasty mandarin of the 1800s, a relatively obscure county magistrate, expressed his shock at rural China's growing poverty and corruption by sitting down to write a critical history of Chinese taxes. In good Mencian fashion, he assumed a connection between such social pathologies and taxes. Pursuing the genealogy of rural China's suffering, the mandarin found much of it lurking in imperial China's three great bouts of top-down tax rationalizations: by Yang Yan in the eighth century; by the Grand Secretary Zhang Juzheng (1525–1582) in the sixteenth century; and by the Yongzheng emperor in the early 1700s. The imperial tax-reform cycle in China had accelerated, in this picture. Eight centuries had come between Yang Yan and Zhang Juzheng, but only one and a half centuries between Zhang and the Yongzheng emperor. What this implied to the nineteenth-century mandarin, who saw it in moral and sociological terms, was that the Chinese bureaucratic system's self-renewal through the particular solution of cyclical tax reforms was running into diminishing returns.

Each reform at the top, by confiscating more of local governments' discretionary funds, had forced the local governments to invent more surcharges that central governments would later try to confiscate in yet another turn of the screw. As the county magistrate saw it, the corruption of local governments was an almost inevitable response to their cyclical beggaring, by the Chinese central government, in the name of administrative reason.[11] In this perspective the Tang tax revolution did not portend a modern commercial revolution; it and its successor reforms over the centuries worked to create the more familiar contemporary China of shallow taxpayer compliance, networks of collusion between government officials at various levels, and cronyism.[12]

Yet the nineteenth-century county magistrate who criticized the unintended effects of administrative reason was part of the phenomenon he was analyzing. Exemplifying the conversion of political problems into administrative ones, he did not see the Chinese central government as directly beggaring local social interests or local social classes; he saw it as beggaring its own administrative units, the local counties. This was a more comfortably apolitical way of perceiving the central government's tax aggrandizements. The state could describe its confiscations of local funds as "restoring them to the public domain" *(gui gong)*. Its elite critics could demand that the confiscations be halted by being "restored to the people" *(gui min)*. But the detachment of this postfeudal administrative language from more specific social or political actors obscured the conflict between the monarchy and local interests as much as it heightened consciousness of it.

Of course this could be seen as a gain for political stability, even if it also illustrated the limits of bureaucratic rationality. Why, a complaining Chinese liberal asked rhetorically in 1947 (in an article that was reprinted in China in 1999), in the long history of the Chinese empire, did Chinese taxpayers not behave like English ones in demanding "the right to speak"? The absence of a society independent of the Chinese state was the answer he wanted. But the reinvention of political issues as administrative ones, in the precociously modern viewpoint of the mandarin ideal, may have had something to do with it.[13]

The political theory of the mandarinates analyzed the hazards of this sort of managerial consciousness. Western writers have only begun to do so relatively recently. In one of the most brilliant books that ever addressed the bureaucratic conversion of political problems into administrative ones (*Ideology and Utopia*, 1929), Karl Mannheim argued that the chief hazard of the narrowly administrative rationality of the Prussian bureaucrats whom he knew so well was that it would blind them to the dangers of the irrational forces operating beyond their particular realm of action, for example Nazis and other revolutionaries.[14] But the longer if more limited east Asian experiment with forms of postfeudal bureaucratic rule demonstrates some of the other risks that were equally acute if less dramatic. One of the big ones was the accumulation of apathy, or of nonconfrontational forms of alienation, at the base of the political system, as the superstructure tried to press its managerial techniques of rational control.

By the seventeenth and eighteenth centuries the nonconfrontational alienation of the "low" from the "high" had become a major anxiety in mandarinate thought, especially in China. Gu Yanwu (1613–1682) was a crucial exponent of what Philip Kuhn has called the "pessimism" of Chinese mandarins about the existence of civic virtue in the Chinese people.[15] Attacking the proliferating layers of supervisory administrative agents in China's provinces, Gu Yanwu famously proposed that state power could be made more meaningful at the local level by a sort of voluntary neofeudal blood transfusion for its bureaucracy. The popular apathy and alienation could be ended, Gu thought, if the spirit of feudalism, with all feudalism's preordained social ties, could be injected into the postfeudal bureaucratic structure. Gu's preferred method for doing this was to allow county magistrates to hold their positions for life (after a trial period) and to recommend their sons to succeed them, even while officials above the county continued to rotate on a temporary, nonhereditary basis as exemplars of a purer meritocratic dynamic.[16] Gu's proposed duality of the feudal and the bureaucratic principles makes an interesting parallel to the proposals today by European thinkers to rescue the European Union—a China-sized unit—by sanctioning a duality of community allegiances, both the traditional local ones and the new supranational ones.[17]

The false notion upon which the nonhereditary mandarinates were based, Gu implied, was that there could be forms of "public spiritedness" that were more than the sum of kinship-based selfishnesses. Limited refeudalization of the state administration would acknowledge this; but Gu's admiration for feudalism came from pure rational calculation of a mandarinal kind, without any of the nostalgia for ancient aristocratic pomp and circumstance such as might be found in European romanticism. Perhaps the best way of imagining a contemporary Western equivalent of Gu would be to think of a political critic who recommended saving capitalism by implanting a revived precapitalist Christianity within it, in order to soften its self-destructive rationalism and give it more emotional ballast.

Mandarinal anxieties about popular apathy in China mounted in the century after Gu's death. Wang Huizu (1731–1807), a county magistrate, demanded that the public business of government, such as the hearing of lawsuits, be made accessible to spectators, so that bystanders would feel involved. The pages of Wang's well-known 1793 guidebook to Chinese local government bristle with observations about the lack of interest of ordinary people in government laws or in state religious cults. Wang preached the need for county magistrates to resolve the estrangement of the people they governed by hiring phalanxes of local teenaged interpreters; such interpreters could then be used to help them investigate the masses, who were said to be like a foreign country riddled with strange taboos.[18]

As it complained about popular apathy about state affairs, the language of such Chinese political theory sounded little like the language of the political thought of eighteenth-century Europe. But it did have a resemblance to the language of more contemporary Western works, like the endless articles about low voter interest in journals like *Public Opinion Quarterly,* or books with titles like *Why Americans Hate Politics.*[19] Until the French Revolution, the dominant political worry in Europe might be said to have been that human political skills could not construct a political order artificial enough, or socially autonomous enough, to avoid being destroyed by sectarian religious passions. (Hence Thomas Hobbes's faith in the "artificial will" of the new sort of state he called the "Leviathan.") In imperial China, and perhaps to a lesser degree in Vietnam and Korea, the corresponding fear was that the political order was always about to become too artificial. Europe was protected for a long time against political apathy of the modern type, not just by its warring religious interests and their armies, but by the remarkable shortness of distance between its early modern "confessional" states (such as Anglican England or Protestant Prussia), which emerged at the end of the religious wars, and its modern nationalist states. Indeed, as the jingoistic Christian clergy of World War One battlefields suggest, the "confessional" and nationalist states merged.

There were no religious wars of the European kind in the east Asian mandarinates, to keep their politics "hot." East Asian political theorists discovered, earlier than European ones, that in polities where the principle of administrative utility gains, and the older personalized feudal loyalty ideals outside the family weaken, the emotional implication of the people in their political system may decline, even if there are no taxpayer revolts of the sort Westernized Chinese liberals now vainly look for in Chinese history. In 1995 a shrewd critic of the contemporary Brussels-ruled, bureaucratized European Union complained that Europe was "too large and too nebulous a concept around which to forge any convincing human community," and that such an "oversized transnational unit" would suffer a "perennial democratic deficit."[20] Substitute "solidarity deficit" for "democratic deficit" in this argument, and it would serve very well to describe what was, for centuries, a central issue in the political theory of imperial China, which was as large as Europe.

All this suggests that Yang Yan's Tang dynasty tax reform of more than twelve centuries ago was not just a landmark in world history because it was a first step toward the global conversion to market-based political systems. It was also a landmark because it was an early omen of the way attempted top-down bureaucratic rationalizations, however unsuccessful they might be in practice, could eventually devitalize the involvement of local communities in their government, causing the nonconfrontational alienation, or estrangement between high and low as Wang Huizu put it in 1793, that corrupt local clerks signified for Chinese political thinkers, and that apathetic voters signify for us. Until very recently, Western political theory surely had—in comparative terms—an impoverished awareness of this particular type of developmental risk.

In the later Chinese empire the spectacular expansion of commerce, and of merchant influence, threatened the further undoing of land reform prospects and Mencian tax principles. By the 1700s the emperor of China had become dependent for extra-budgetary revenues upon big merchants who could appropriately be called commercial "rent-seekers" (users of their government connections, and licenses, for business advantages), if not yet crony capitalists. The salt merchants who underwrote the Qianlong reign as its investment managers and cash cows paid for much of that emperor's military activity in central Asia and Taiwan.[21] Administrative theories of poverty relief could not remain immune to this commercial expansion, or to the necessary decline of direct state control of the more complex economy. Some high government officials even abandoned the bedrock idea that bad politics caused poverty, blaming changes in popular consumer culture instead.[22] Some high scholar-officials (Qin Huitian, 1702–1764) argued that poverty was not a question of politically created scarcity at all, but merely of inefficient distribution. The wealth of the empire was not circulating properly. The secret of the eradication of poverty did not lie in land equalization programs, but in full acceptance of the legitimate use of money to integrate the Chinese empire's welfare objectives. This could be done by the mobilization of the wealth of rich households, through government sales to them of various privileges, and its redistribution to famine-relief granaries and to the poor. In this scheme the rich were endowed with a useful transformative power, rather like that of charitable foundations or NGOs: they were depicted as a state-directed asset, ready to supplement state power, rather than as an historic social class.[23]

But east Asia's archetypal welfare ideals did not suffer the same meltdown in Korea and Vietnam as they did in eighteenth-century China. By that time the "equal fields" communitarian ideal, which was at odds with the more market-driven utilitarianism of the great Chinese tax-reform cycles, enjoyed greater credibility among Vietnamese and Korean mandarins than it did among Chinese ones. There were many possible reasons. In negative terms, this could have reflected the circumstance that weaker states, as the contemporary world shows, often have more difficulty than strong ones in making shifts in their functions and reducing state responsibilities. It could also have reflected Vietnamese and Korean imprisonment in a more slowly moving, less commercialized evolutionary process. Korean reformers tried but failed to create an economy and a social elite like that of Qing China, Palais suggests, because prejudice against commerce had become too deeply ingrained in the "*yangban* psyche."[24] Vietnam, despite a significant participation in South China Sea trade, never developed an indigenous merchant class of its own comparable to the Chinese and Japanese ones; and Chinese coinage may have made up the majority of the money in circulation in Vietnam for most of its history.

But it is dangerously reductive to take an economic determinist view of fashions in political theory. The more pertinent issue is the way in which the mandarinates' sizes affected such fashions. Korean and Vietnamese administrative hierarchies were less tall than China's. The proliferation of officials whose primary task was to manage other officials, rather than directly to address local policy needs, was less obvious. Their mandarinates' smaller sizes apparently encouraged Vietnamese and Korean elite thinkers to assume that there would be more public support at the local level for micromodeling land-redistribution schemes engineered from above by government officials. The assumption that state salvationism of this type was only possible in smaller (and poorer) mandarinates could even be said to have been an Asian bureaucratic echo of the European belief—exemplified by Rousseau—that freedom could only flourish in small states. But it overlooked the fact that the very structure of a government of circulating bureaucrats with limited terms constricted officials' social knowledge of the "low"—local interests—even as it increased their objectivity with respect to such interests. Despite their smaller sizes, there is little evidence of a significantly stronger connection between social trust and confidence in government institutions in the Vietnamese and Korean mandarinates.

Even so, the rulers of Vietnam in the 1700s and 1800s, acting on the apparent belief that Yang Yan was the product of a purely Chinese administrative decadence, rejected the entire logic of imperial China's tax-reform cycles. In 1723 the Trinh family lord who ruled northern Vietnam announced that he had made an historical examination of past political land management in east Asia. Repudiating the past ten centuries of Chinese tax reforms, Trinh Cuong proposed that the best tax system of all, and the one whose purposes could most readily be understood by the Vietnamese people, was the pre–Yang Yan, early Tang dynasty's three-part "land-labor-household" tax (*to dung dieu* in Vietnamese). This was precisely the tax that Tang China itself had abandoned nearly a thousand years before. Trinh Cuong tried to reintroduce this early medieval tax formula into north Vietnam, which at the time was a checkerboard of different regional tax rates; he and some of his successors (notably Trinh Doanh, ruler 1740–1767) evidently hoped to make it part of a restored "equal fields" system in the Red River delta.

Unfortunately, the actual north Vietnamese tax reforms failed. They got caught up in a microengineering zeal that aimed to compensate for the depersonalization of personal accountability in tax collections in China, feared because it led to a more general depersonalization of ties between the political order and its people. In the end, the Vietnamese tax reformers overcompensated. Tax inspectors in Tonkin were sent out to classify all farm lands according to three categories of fertility, each of which would be assessed a different tax quota; even Buddhist temples were given different degrees of tax immunity for their lands, depending upon whether the temples were "very famous," "famous," or just ordinary. Such an ambitious restructuring of taxable resources reflected a characteristic mandarin belief in the convenience of bureaucratically produced space such as could not have occurred to tax administrators in a more feudal society. But with its opportunities for bureaucratic subjectivism, it disturbed local popular feelings every bit as much as the very different tax policies of China's major reformers led to alienation there.[25]

Korean mandarin thinkers, like Vietnamese ones, also appear to have refused to go as far as their counterparts in the later Chinese empire in abandoning the explanation of poverty as politically distorted scarcity. Yu Hyongwon (1622–1673) might as well have served as the inspiration for Trinh Cuong, by agreeing that the early Tang "equal fields" and tax systems came as close as was practicable to the ancient "three dynasties" ideal; Yi Ik (1681–1763), whose lifetime overlapped with Trinh Cuong's, proposed that Korea revive even the terminology of the early Tang land and tax systems, as part of a gradual equalization of land tenure among the Korean people; Chong Yagyong (1762–1836) even thought that the ancient "well-field" system itself was within reach in Korea, provided a "long time" was spent first reviving the less ambitious "equal fields" of the early Chinese empire.[26]

The difference was that Choson Korea's rulers never attempted an experimental reenactment of early Tang taxes as exacting as the attempted north Vietnamese tax reforms of the early 1700s. *Yangban* landowners constituted a formidable barrier against major schemes of land reform such as no Vietnamese landlord class could ever be; this probably accounts also for the more gradualistic blueprints for land reform that Korean *Sirhak* reformers wanted to see put into play. But like their Vietnamese colleagues, Korean reformers still wanted to legislate happiness for peasants through the greater equalization of farmland. In the mandarin world of both, tax policy remained part of the more general administrative pursuit of salvation. So did the way in which a combination of philosophical ambition and administrative power, expressed in a "ten thousand capabilities" view of taxes, allowed for no more than a shallow stability.

The Recurrence of Solidarity Deficits

A solidarity deficit is usually seen in the West as a modern problem, attributable to a rights-oriented liberal individualism whose preoccupation was to loosen feudal bonds in early modern Europe. But the examinations-based bureaucracies of the mandarinates, and the distance of bureaucratic planners from local needs, had also weakened vertical ties between rulers and ruled in them, and generated a solidarity deficit, earlier in history.

In China, whose size made the problem most severe, there were numerous proposals to fight the deficit by creating new kinds of vertical ties (apart from the examinations) between governments and locally based corporatisms (families and lineages). In the early 1800s Wei Yuan charged that existing lineage charitable institutions (schools, granaries, cemeteries) were weak substitutes for the more feudal organizations that had once regulated social welfare; his solution was a government-led amalgamation of Chinese lineages into superlineages, which the government would then direct. One of Wei's contemporaries, a Beijing academician, went even further. He demanded that the ministry of rites centralize control over all lineage registers in China, dividing them into five categories; after a bureaucratic purification process, the newly rationalized lineages could then be given state-enforced powers of ostracism and genealogical excommunication, and the social fragmentation of a political order based on circulating bureaucrats would end.[27] But this dream of turning lineage patriarchs into state policemen only showed how far China had moved away from feudalism toward bureaucracy.

Significantly, however, all three mandarinates shared one Neo-Confucian institution whose purpose, in part, was to revitalize if not re-emotionalize local political behavior and strengthen the communitarian understanding of the "self," in contrast to the less socially embodied selves of circulating officials. That institution was the village covenant or community compact (Chinese: *xiangyue*; Korean: *hyangyak*; Vietnamese: *huong uoc*).

The community compacts were locally organized associations designed to educate, to provide famine relief and other forms of mutual aid, and to maintain neighborhood security and punish uncivil or criminal behavior. If they stopped short of directly functioning as mechanisms for the reinforcing of vertical ties to the state, their locally centered ideological conditioning processes and rituals were nonetheless clearly intended to block the spread of civic apathy of the sort the three mandarinates feared. The compacts originated in China in the Song dynasty, in the eleventh century. They probably began to become important in Korea by the 1500s; the original Chinese Lü Family community compact was translated into the Korean vernacular in 1517. The first known Vietnamese community compact, of a village in north central Vietnam, can be dated to the first half of the 1600s.[28] The compacts appear to have worked least well over the centuries in China, where they were presumably most needed. The subject is underresearched, but they seem ironically to have flourished better in Korea and in northern and north central Vietnam, whose bureaucratic cultures were correspondingly weaker and where there was less need for them.

As omens of what is modern, the compacts, like so much else in the mandarinates, are ambiguous. On the one hand, as the German scholar Monika Ubelhör has pointed out, the compacts were originally designed in the Song dynasty as substitutes for the feudalism that was disappearing. Their purpose was to manufacture a post-aristocratic community consciousness in the crucial period when scholar-officials were replacing the Tang dynasty's "great families of old."[29] On the other hand, as artificial forms of corporatism that served state purposes but were not directly controlled by the state, they were hardly expressions of that independent civil society that so many Western liberals believe to be critical to the rise and maintenance of a modern political consciousness.

But the historical conditioning of this belief raises questions about its universality. Centuries of religious warfare in Europe stimulated a desperate Western desire to conceptualize a separation of state from society, as part of the struggle to separate religion from politics. The much more recent history of Europe has become more east Asian: labor unions and employer groups have been integrated into state planning in many countries, making enough "interweaving" of society and government to weaken the importance of the distinction.[30] The postwar British term "quango," for quasi-autonomous non-governmental organization, expresses the waning of the distinction in major policymaking realms in the West—outside the United States. ("Gongos," government-organized non-governmental organizations, go even further.) The three east Asian mandarinates' community compacts were Neo-Confucian quangos, not necessarily as much at odds with modern institutional development as might be assumed.

Each mandarinate vernacularized the compacts differently. The Korean compacts appear to have been more concerned than Chinese ones with the punitive defense of status differentiation. Yi I's famous Haeju covenant of 1577 went further than the medieval Chinese ones known to us in marginalizing people like secondary sons and slaves in local seating arrangements and rituals; providing more severe punishments for slave misbehavior; and in general, stressing the elite's disciplinary powers over non-elite society.[31] That the academy-based literati who designed the Korean compacts felt such a strong need to do this suggests that Korea had not escaped the east Asian tension between meritocratic examinations and the ambition to recapture fading feudal techniques of social mobilization, even if Korean literati were better placed than their Chinese counterparts to control the tension.

In Vietnam, unlike Choson Korea, the literati were not based in academies or segregated as much from commoners. Vietnamese village compacts were devised largely by the literate men within the villages who made up the village associations known as "orthodox culture" (*tu van*, from a phrase in the Confucian Analects) groups. Because their authors were more directly immersed in village life than the Neo-Confucian literati of China and Korea, it was easier for village culture to permeate the compacts. Moreover, Vietnamese peasants of the sixteenth, seventeenth, and eighteenth centuries were undoubtedly more mobile than Korean commoners, and therefore in a better bargaining position with local elites. Not only did Vietnam have a moving frontier until 1802, much later than Korea, but identity tags for peasants, such as the ones enacted in Choson Korea in the 1400s, were not seriously considered by Vietnamese rulers before the end of the 1700s, when the rebel Tay-son emperor embraced the idea without being able to impose it. So although Vietnamese governments tried to use the covenants as local instruments for stimulating Confucian activism, the Vietnamese covenants were more likely than the Korean or Chinese ones to be captured from below. Some known Vietnamese compacts even focused on the rules for hunting wild animals, others on primitive New Year's blood oaths against cheating or stealing inside the village.[32]

But for all the variety of the east Asian mandarinates' community compacts from the 1500s to the 1800s, world history shows us their important common feature. Both Europeans and east Asians in this period were busy trying to construct artificial communities with clear rules. The types of communities that were constructed—legally muscular "Leviathan" states in Europe, apathy-fighting rural covenants in China, Korea, and Vietnam —indicate what was thought to be missing in each civilization.

The European political order suffered from too little superordinate political authority with the capacity to control religious warfare, and too much independent communitarian enthusiasm of a lethal kind. The European wars between Catholics and Protestants not only led to public mass killings of the sort we associate today with Rwanda, but also produced bloody struggles featuring Catholic Leagues led by aristocrats, Protestant assemblies led by nobles, and militarized religious sects, all of which reinvented community power in ways that undermined weak European governments. Such religious turmoil in Europe in the 1500s and 1600s, in circumstances where feudal forms of authority still survived, ensured that communitarian apathy, or alienation of a nonconfrontational kind, would not be a problem there. Discordant communitarianisms that were too strong were the threat.

In the east Asian mandarinates, however, the very real if limited success of the Confucian civil religion, combined with bureaucratic recruitment systems that partly depersonalized loyalties, implied that the political order had, or might have, a deficiency of communitarian enthusiasm. The response to this deficiency included celebrated community compacts like Wang Yangming's south Jiangxi covenant of 1520, written in the same century as the Saint Bartholomew's Day religious massacres in France. Wang's covenant tried to inculcate a commitment to good collective behavior in its villagers by leading them in a series of chorused oral declarations and choreographed questions and answers, accompanied by drum beatings and wine pourings.[33] It was almost like a state-sponsored Neo-Confucian gospel hour. The mandarinates had inevitably witnessed the decline of those fully aristocratic codes of reciprocity in which, as the Chinese formulation had it, the people "ate their princes' food"; the emotional resonances of national politics at the local level were too weak, rather than too strong as in Europe. But this was an achievement for which many Europeans in Wang Yangming's century would have yearned.

The Restless Ghost of Mencius

Of course modern representative democracies, which the mandarinates were not, cope better with the hazard of apathy or weak political commitments at the local level, even if they do not escape it. For the mandarinates, if managerial manipulation exacerbated the weakness, managerial remedies were nonetheless the only cure. In this respect the belief that bad administration created poverty, and good administration could end it, probably had multiple functions.

No matter whether the economy was prosperous or depressed, commercial or agrarian, the belief survived. Scholar-officials refused to let go of it. In the early 1800s, writing in a very poor northern Vietnam that was trying to recover from civil war, the supreme Vietnamese mandarin Phan Huy Chu asserted that it was precisely at the outset of a dynasty, when everybody was poor and there were few rich people around to resist a return to the ideals of the ancient "three dynasties," that an equal fields system could be "easily" introduced. The poor would be glad to have their "sickness" cured by the state-enforced equalization of landholding.[34] This point of view brought Phan Huy Chu very close to an unintentional anticipation of the Maoist theories in the next century that the people's poverty would make a revolution easier.

But in the age of extravagance in eighteenth-century China, whose teahouses were full of big-spending merchants, the belief also remained unextinguished in bureaucratic politics, even if it had become far weaker. Was it really only "poor Confucian literati" who "constantly" advocated the imposition of a compulsory equal fields system in China, as the Qianlong emperor once publicly and sarcastically supposed? Hardly: in 1743 a high Manchu official and former director of the government grain tribute system (Guzong, 1685–1755) proposed that a government-designed equal fields system be tried out as an experiment in Huaian prefecture, Jiangsu, where whatever administrative excesses and unrest it produced could be confined to one place. And even Qianlong was anxious not to make a frontal attack on the redistributive version of welfare politics. He looked for a way out by suggesting that the "surplus" wealth of rich people was simply not yet large enough in the 1700s to remedy the insufficiencies of the poor.[35] From Vietnam to Korea, the faith in a legislated end to poverty kept being recycled, if never realized.

And there were surely other reasons for its underlying resilience besides moral conscience and the effect the examination systems had in reconciling the study of ancient ideals with training for administrative positions in the present. Government officials, prisoners of a tight labor market for good bureaucratic posts that an emperor like Qianlong publicly spoke of having to "dredge" periodically, had to gain their self-respect through a myth of transformative action of which they were the instruments; they could no longer gain it just by embodying aristocratic virtues. Advocacy of the "three dynasties" ideal also functioned as a means of escape from bureaucratic performance standards that had become too stereotyped, too textual, and too cut off from real experience. The irony was that the ideal itself was largely a textual one, and also suffered from a lack of input by local social and political actors.

Given its multiple functions, this part of the classical heritage has not been completely submerged by the fall of the old order in much of east Asia. The notion that poverty is politically created, and can be reduced by administrative means, may be old-fashioned by east Asian standards, if not by those of the West, but it is not out of date. In the spring of 1988 Vietnam, whose agriculture was beginning to be decollectivized, teetered on the edge of famine. There were many insider critics of this situation. One of the most eloquent ones was Nguyen Khac Vien, a French-educated doctor and a distinguished elder of the Vietnamese communist movement. In September 1988 this aged communist chastised the cadres of his own government for destroying a perfectly good market-garden economy in his home region near Vinh by their Stalinist planning obsession with grain. Anxious to remind these cadres that Vietnamese malnutrition was caused by bad government policies, not by storms or a scarcity of farmland, Vien reached for the most effective rhetorical weapon he could find. That weapon was not Marx, but Mencius.

Specifically, in 1988 Nguyen Khac Vien called the Hanoi politburo's attention (in the party newspaper) to the dramatic confrontations between Mencius and King Hui of Liang, about twenty-three centuries earlier. As any classically educated Vietnamese person would have known, in the text Mencius had told King Hui of Liang that there would be no famines or food shortages if the state refrained from interfering with peasants' farming practices; maintained granaries for famine relief; kept taxes light; and restrained its courtiers and other members of its elite from overconsumption of the harvest, so that entitlements to food could be broadly diffused.[36]

If the ghost of Mencius still stalked the capital city of Vietnam at the end of the twentieth century, it could be because bureaucracy still needed a code of accountability, however ancient, and because the message that bad politics caused poverty seemed very modern, despite its adumbration in this highly feudal text. The possibilities of enhanced state power in the aristocracy-free industrial age in the West now encourage important Western thinkers to explore the theme too. Amartya Sen, the winner of the 1998 Nobel Prize for economics, has become celebrated for his claim that declining entitlement to food, not declining availability of food, is the principal cause of famines; Sen's claim that "starvation deaths can reflect legality with a vengeance" echoes Mencius, even if it is expressed in a very different idiom and assumes the high value of democratic institutions that ancient east Asians could not have understood.[37]

But the real parallel between preindustrial east Asia and the more contemporary industrial world is the shared effort to design a postfeudal welfare state, however much more primitive and limited this effort may have been in east Asia. Such an enterprise is surely a positive one, and inevitable as well, in human history. But it has its hazards. The abstract legalism of industrial welfare states, and the introverted bureaucratic planning and textualization of reality in the mandarinates, both threatened to detach the enterprise from the moral resources and the active solidarities of the people for whom the enterprise was intended. Industrial states have far more complex and democratic antidotes for this detachment than the east Asian mandarins' old self-centered "three dynasties" critique of morally destructive forms of bureaucratic intervention. But we can glimpse some of the hazards of the enterprise at a remarkably early point in east Asian history, long before capitalism created the risks that scholars like Anthony Giddens consider modern. All this adds to the need for new historians' experiments with answers to the question, What time is east Asia?

— 4 —

Mandarin Management Theorists?

In the twentieth century China and Vietnam—North Korea must be excluded from this discussion—turned themselves into militarized republics whose historical kinship was not so obviously with the old mandarinates as with the type of political system the French Revolution and Napoleon first created and Lenin refined. China and Vietnam became states with a dualistic character. They were supposedly the political embodiments of mass nations. But they were also, clearly, managerial instruments designed to transcend the turmoil of the competing interest groups within the mass nations. And at the end of the twentieth century, Chinese and Vietnamese reformers further complicated this dualistic pattern by trying to introduce market economics into formerly collectivized, industrializing blue-collar societies whose insecurities would have been more familiar to Charles Dickens than to Confucius.

On the face of it, therefore, the mandarin ideal was dead. People wearing mandarin gowns and attempting to get government positions by writing poetry examinations were unlikely to reappear. The historical continuity in China and Vietnam, indeed the continuity of what was modern in them, lay not so much in their institutions as in the persistence of a certain kind of crisis. This was the crisis of a bureaucratic subjectivism, much criticized over the centuries by mandarins themselves, which took a totalistic or "ten thousand capabilities" view of its top-down problem-solving capacities at the cost of exaggerating or misunderstanding the actual social demand for them.

This situation was indeed one that the great tragic playwrights would have recognized as a crisis, because of its being integral to the historical makeup of its principal actors, rather than being entirely visited upon them by outsiders. And yet, developments in the now equally bureaucratic outside world did force a new recognition of some of the virtues of the old east Asian mandarin tradition. Such a recognition was strengthened by the example of non-Leninist South Korea, which began to supply advanced ideas about civil service examinations to China. If this was not quite an east Asian man-bites-dog story, it was nonetheless an interesting reversal of the patterns of the preindustrial circulation of political inspirations in east Asia. Western business schools' management theory also sporadically called attention to the virtues of preindustrial east Asian personnel development techniques, agreeing that they had had surprisingly modern qualities. In addition, Western management theory suggested ways of going much further than preindustrial east Asians ever had in converting acutely political questions into seemingly less contentious problems of rational organization. In that respect it was far from uninvolved in the crisis, which had acquired a global dimension.

Schizoid Views of Mandarinism

Heinrich Heine famously commented in the early 1800s that any future German revolution would not take place any more gently or pleasantly for having been preceded by the Kantian critique, or by Fichtean transcendental idealism. A similar prophecy in east Asia at the same time, that revolutions in China or Vietnam or Korea would not be made any more gentle for having been preceded by mandarinates, would have been equally appropriate. Mandarins became important scapegoats for the humiliations that eastern Asia suffered at the hands of Western and Japanese colonialism after 1840. All the encyclopedic handbooks and elaborate treatises on government that the scholar-officials of the three mandarinates had produced before 1840 came to seem more like embarrassments than like useful inventories of important theory, at least to the intellectual elites and revolutionaries who experienced the humiliations. Their reaction was undoubtedly at least as extreme as that of the cultured Europeans who found it painful to read classical works like the *Iliad*, with their focus on soldiers and soldiering, after the slaughter of Europe's World War One trench warfare.

Liang Qichao, a particularly angry critic, began the critical assault on the legacy of the mandarinates in 1896. He asserted that the civil service examinations had been nothing more than a convenient weapon by which despotic emperors strengthened themselves, stifled independent critical theory and dissent, and kept the people stupid. In behaving this way, such rulers were like householders who tied up their own servants in order to prevent the servants from attacking them.[1] Liang's dramatic image, of the mandarinates' rulers as paranoid house owners who had successfully postponed evolution, was hard to escape in the politically haunted decades after 1896 (or by some social scientists now). Yet it is very difficult for even the most scrupulous professional historians to answer fully the question of who actually controlled the examinations upon which the mandarinates were based. It is fairly clear that their questions and curricular material were conditioned by the views, not just of emperors, but of hundreds of examiners and "checking" officials who shaped them by a subtle and variegated repertoire of maneuvers over which they apparently had full discretionary command.

The great irony of the examinations-as-the-instrument-of-despotism thesis was that, in its despair at the absence of a tradition of political theory similar to the Western one, it failed either to recognize or to match the profundity of the criticisms of the system that mandarins themselves had made before the mandarinates declined. These criticisms had included the foreboding that meritocracies subverted themselves by creating standardized testing monocultures; and the fear (as in Gu Yanwu) that political systems based on circulating, nonhereditary officials might run the risk of becoming too socially abstracted or emotionally inert to generate adequate support for themselves, especially during a crisis. Equally ironically, the minority of important figures in east Asian revolutionary circles who resisted the trend of denigration and praised the mandarinates, or at least their examinations, were in many instances—like Sun Yat-sen—complete outsiders to mandarin culture.

At their extreme, in post-1949 China, attacks upon old-fashioned mandarins became part of what Geremie Barmé so aptly calls a literature of "self-loathing," such as might paradoxically reaffirm China's sense of national uniqueness.[2] Authors of books with titles like "the defects of Chinese people" proposed that the rank-consciousness of centuries of Chinese officialdom had now infected the various sectors of contemporary Chinese life, contaminating even the leaders of writers' associations, business corporation executives, the principals and professors of universities, and the heads of student associations and of villager organizations. It was claimed that if bureaucratic culture had originally been a Chinese contribution to humankind, it had by now exhausted all its positive functions in human development; Mao Zedong was wrong to see capitalism as the major threat to the socialist revolution in China when he should have seen that the real danger was bureaucratic culture.[3] In October 2000 President Jiang Zemin told a Chinese communist party "work style" conference that leading party cadres were still "prisoners" of the bureaucratic "departmentalism" of Chinese preindustrial civilization. To Jiang, such departmentalism included the practice of fraud and trickery, the buying and selling of government offices and their assets, the pursuit of individual status, and a worldly-wise playing for safety.[4]

In Vietnam, whatever merits the old mandarinate had possessed were obscured, between 1885 and 1954, by the French Indochina colonial regime's effort to use the Vietnamese mandarin service ethic to suit its own ends. The French even preserved the preindustrial civil service examinations in Vietnam until 1919, some fourteen years after the Chinese ones had been abolished. This was part of their strategy of "association" of European imperial control with the moral authority of indigenous scholar-officials. In 1950, four years before Dienbienphu, at the last gasp of their struggle to stay in Vietnam, the French Indochina Civic Training Directorate was busying itself sponsoring the publication of laudatory books about major Vietnamese scholar-officials of the past (such as Nguyen Cong Tru, 1778–1858) who had supposedly specialized in politically tranquilizing expositions of Confucian harmony. When he was still in the forests fighting a guerrilla war against the French, and had no bureaucracy, Ho Chi Minh nonetheless wrote a tract about the need to reform Vietnamese communist party cadres' work styles (October 1947) so as to avoid "bureaucratic" remoteness.

Of course the parallels between the Chinese and Vietnamese rejections of mandarinism are not exact. Not having as grandiose a sense of national uniqueness as the Chinese, Vietnamese writers have had correspondingly less need for "self-loathing" literary exercises. Moreover, too many Vietnamese revolutionaries had mandarin ancestors. In 1990 UNESCO canonized Ho Chi Minh, who was one of them, as a global cultural luminary, a fairly unusual fate for a Marxist-Leninist politician, in part because of what UNESCO perceived as Ho's mandarin sensibilities. This inspired the appearance of books about Ho, in Vietnam itself, which praised his Confucian spirituality and showed a bespectacled Ho reading inscriptions at the temple of Nguyen Trai, the preeminent Vietnamese scholar-official of the

1400s.[5] Other Vietnamese books of the 1990s celebrated the pedigrees of the Vietnamese mandarin families before 1802 who had produced three to six generations' worth of metropolitan degree-holders in the old civil service examinations. Such books defended their veneration of mandarin families by quoting Hegel to the effect that it was "geniuses" and "great people" who led human progress. Vietnamese newspaper writers even demanded that the Vietnamese government build an "education museum," similar to the French Pantheon, to honor the nearly three thousand Vietnamese metropolitan degree winners who had triumphed in the old examinations between the eleventh century and 1919.[6] In 1991 history came full circle. The Hanoi council of ministers ordered the "restoration" of a national system of civil servants whose members would be ranked, salaried, and recruited through public examinations.

Nor was China able to escape the pull of remandarinization, with all its political ambiguities. Deng Xiaoping argued in August 1980 that China's baneful bureaucratic culture was really the product of the discredited pre-1978 command economy; it was not just a madness left over from the preindustrial empire. Deng made it clear that China's best cadres needed a new promotions "ladder" in order to demonstrate their excellence, and that there would be "very many" positions and professional titles in the future whose distribution would depend upon success in examinations. In the 1980s Chinese provincial and municipal governments began to publish personnel recruitment and management journals bearing titles like "People of Talent Universe" (*Rencai tiandi,* in Qinghai) or "People of Talent Information Journal" (*Rencai xinxi bao,* in Shenyang). Provisional regulations for a new examinations-based civil service took effect in China in October 1993. By 1995 some Chinese historians had become bold enough to hail the old preindustrial civil service examinations as China's "fifth great discovery," after the compass, gunpowder, paper, and printing.[7]

Other habits of the mandarinate showed signs of returning with the "people of talent" cult. Before he was ousted as party general secretary in 1987, Hu Yaobang demanded that younger party cadres remold themselves through reading, by pledging themselves to read two hundred million words' worth of books as part of their self-cultivation for reform. Embarrassed by their complaints that such a program would take fifty years to complete, at a rate of four million words a year, Hu Sheng, the president of the academy of social sciences, responded soothingly that it could actually be done in twenty years. Only one-quarter of the books in the program needed to be closely read theoretical works; the remainder could be novels, histories, and travel texts that would not require "straightening one's clothes and sitting properly," but could be consumed quickly at a clip of fifty thousand words per hour.[8]

The traditional mandarinal belief that with book-based omniscience, the entire world might be administrable, was plainly not dead in post-1978 China and Vietnam. It had an obvious if elastic affinity with the Enlightenment belief, at the heart of Western modernity, that the rationalist use of mathematical and scientific thinking procedures could make the entire world calculable. Hu Yaobang and Hu Sheng were making a neotraditional invocation of the old Neo-Confucian insistence that the exploration of principles required the reading of books; almost to the point of parody, they were making themselves into the successors of the preindustrial mandarins like Cheng Duanli (1271–1345) who had written famous treatises planning daily schedules of reading for youths that could reconcile thorough reading of the sages with the rapid reading of less important texts.

But the conviction that a mastery of texts facilitates a mastery of life, hazardous as many critics feared it to be in the mandarinates, is more hazardous now. It is being imposed upon societies with much understandably defensive anxiety about the return of bureaucratic elitism marking the end of lower-class revolutions. In the summer of 2000 the head of the Chinese personnel ministry was forced to show that China's new civil service tests, in the seven years since 1993, had smashed "status" boundaries, rather than restoring them, by recruiting more than two thousand peasants and ten thousand or more people of "worker" background into the civil service. He added nervously that China must still greatly increase the "trickling down power" of its civil service tests.[9]

The concern about the domestic "trickling down power" of the new civil service examinations suggested that complex international pressures at the elite level, not native grassroots nostalgia for the past, might be the real cause of the examinations' revival. China and Vietnam both needed to imagine more attractive futures for their intelligentsias, given their acute brain drains to more industrially advanced countries. (Chinese sources calculated that of the three hundred thousand or so Chinese students who completed study abroad between 1978 and 1997, only one-third had returned to China, a much lower rate than the average two-thirds rate of return of the overseas students of other "developing" counties.)[10] Perhaps even more worrisome, the personnel-management practices of foreign corporations in places like Shanghai and Ho Chi Minh City competed only too well with those of party and government organizations. That made it difficult for state bureaucratic organs to recruit the best and brightest university and middle school graduates in the societies they supposedly ruled. In Shanghai municipal officials publicly expressed their admiration for the "innovativeness" of the techniques for mobilizing "people of talent" used by foreign businesses like Microsoft, which allegedly gave their Chinese employees "trust" and "esteem" that domestic institutions could not match.[11] In this way an American multinational corporation became co-opted into serving as a new sort of external reference for the validation of something quite old: the centuries of struggle by post-aristocratic east Asian mandarins to win types of respect for themselves that were not directly attached to hereditary forms of power or ownership.

Perhaps economic globalization was simply giving local cultures, including the mandarinal one, new meaning. Mandarinism, in all its potentialities and its hazards, was not displaced; it had always been too implicitly modern for that; it was rather being reinvented on an expanding transnational foundation. The old mandarin ideal had been a cross-cultural project, involving as it did Korean and Vietnamese energies as well as Chinese ones. Now the replacement of old collectivist slogans like "the socialization of the means of production" by neotraditional ones like the "innovativeness of people-of-talent arrangements" signaled an enlarged and accelerated cross-cultural reproduction of at least some mandarin values, but based now upon idealist interpretations of Microsoft's success as much as of Mencius.

The result was an increasingly polyglot managerial language whose superficial cosmopolitanism apparently disarmed some of its natural antagonists, while preserving all the risks of traditional mandarinism. One Chinese researcher estimated that between 1983 and 1999 almost one thousand books were published in China on the subject of "leadership science." Such books characteristically combined Confucius and Sunzi with Lenin and Mao, and then with Lincoln, Napoleon, Einstein, and Frederick Winslow Taylor. The juxtaposition of Confucius and Taylor, in particular, meant a marriage of the east Asian historical subconscious with the supposedly liberal West's twentieth-century obsession with the business organization, not the individual, as the epitome of rationality.[12] But Western books about management did the same thing, helping to legitimize the east Asian ones. Peter Senge's 1990 bestseller, *The Fifth Discipline*, written by a specialist at MIT's Sloan School of Management, quite deliberately exalted the old east Asian mandarin ideal of "learning" (as constant, endless study and practice), using it as an antidote to the alleged fragmentation of Western business executives' thinking. This was not very different in intent from Hu Yaobang and Hu Sheng. The Chinese administrators who wished to reform Chinese state-owned enterprises then discussed Senge's "rich" and "sensational" insights, borrowing back his American version of the Chinese "person of talent."[13]

For Chinese and Vietnamese reformers, this mixed managerial thought also had latent functions. At the end of the twentieth century both Chinese and Vietnamese leaders were having obvious difficulty with definitions of the ultimate ends of politics: that is, with imagining political alternatives to Western models of democracy at a time when they remained disinclined fully to embrace such models. In the words of one Chinese village development specialist in 1998, the era of failed collectivism and its aftermath had created a bad policy environment in which party cadres had so corrupted the public sphere, or delegitimized it, that the Chinese people suffered from a "fear-of-cooperation disease" *(konghe zheng)*, even when it came to developing their own village organizations.[14] For state intellectuals, various versions of remandarinization could come to be seen as at least provisional substitutes for the ideal of the public good that Western democracies upheld and that the earlier excesses of the party dictatorships had undermined.

When an examinations-based civil service was reintroduced into Vietnam in May 1991, some Vietnamese thinkers certainly hoped that the civil servants it produced would supply the country with a new mystique of public service, to the point of marginalizing old-fashioned party cadres. One Vietnamese legal specialist, himself a government cadre, boldly contrasted civil servants and party cadres: the former stood for a highly educated and meritocratic social order, whereas the latter stood for a primitive, unspecialized "egalitarianism."[15] Remandarinization's function would be to simulate something like a higher moral authority of the democratic kind without all the risks of political democracy.

South Korean Inspirations

For this reason, utopian views of bureaucracy, rather than "self-loathing" vilifications of the bureaucratic past, were probably the greater danger.

Chinese reform planners must not idealize their administrative "goal models" to the point of lapsing into utopianism, one well-established Chinese economist warned in 1988, sounding as he did so a little like Wang Fuzhi complaining of "ten thousand capabilities" views of tax policy three centuries earlier.[16] But the historical echo, apt in one sense, was deceiving in another. The retreat of Soviet and Maoist pictures of bureaucracy—as an exploitative social stratum opposed to popular interests—allowed for the emergence of a curious precritical appreciation of bureaucracy, often expressed in futurological terms, that detached it not just from previous revolutionary demonizations of it but, more important, from the centuries of critical self-consciousness that bureaucratic government had generated in preindustrial east Asia itself. The result was an historically unwarranted age of innocence about bureaucratic forms, completely divorced from the east Asian heritage of debates about Tang China's ministry of civil appointments or the tactical silences of Vietnamese censors. Skepticism about bureaucracy, than which nothing was more east Asian, now came to be regarded as the luxury of established intelligentsias in rich Western countries. And South Korea—an east Asian industrial society more economically advanced than China and Vietnam—became important as a place, sufficiently removed from past Leninist versions of bureaucracy, upon which Chinese and Vietnamese elites could project their own futurological taste for bureaucracy and from which they could derive lessons about how to rebuild it.

In an address to an October 1992 conference on administration and politics in Seoul, Korea, the longtime director of the Vietnamese Institute of State and Law in Hanoi, Dao Tri Uc, renounced the old Vietnamese communists' Soviet-bloc prejudice that bureaucracy was always an apparatus remote from the masses. The effect of this stereotyped Marxist-Leninist attack on bureaucracy, Uc said, had been to prevent Vietnam from creating what it really needed: a state that could function as an objective "administrative referee" *(tai phan hanh chinh)* in coordinating the country's social and political relations.

Uc's belief in the possibility of an impartial "referee" state remembered little of preindustrial east Asian concerns about how bureaucrats could mediate. Instead it had all the flavor of the innocence of the eighteenth-century Western Enlightenment's view of benevolent historical agency, before gloomy German philosophers had begun to worry (belatedly, by east Asian standards) about the connections between bureaucracy and disenchantment. Because this gloomy German thought is now part of the global echo chamber of ideas, along with American business school reinventions of east Asian mandarin learning theory, Uc had to deal with it in Seoul in 1992. He went out of his way to reject it. For his Korean audience, Uc singled out Karl Mannheim's famous theory (in *Ideology and Utopia*, 1929) that bureaucratic thought crippled its own capacity to understand continuing human irrationalities by its conversion of political problems into administrative ones; he suggested that Mannheim's views were too pessimistic to help Vietnamese reformers in 1992.

What Vietnam really needed, Uc told Koreans, was a new class of "political administrators." They might come from a variety of political parties, or they might come from no political party at all. They would be superior to Vietnamese party politicians because, like the old mandarins, they would have a special education-based understanding of the world. That understanding would originate in their mastery of the information sciences, and thus in the reflexive management of "negotiations" with the different social forces in Vietnam.[17] Inevitably, as this speech showed, veiled proposals for the diminution of party dictatorship in Hanoi (or Beijing) reversed the more standardized Western perceptions of the hazards of modernity, as well as much preindustrial east Asian political theory. At the beginning of the 1800s the Spanish painter Goya famously warned (anticipating Mannheim and Weber and others) that the dream of reason would bring forth monsters. In China and Vietnam two centuries later it was the monsters (failed collectivist experiments) that compelled an awakening of the dream of reason—or at least a covert reawakening of dreams about mandarins.

Dao Tri Uc's use of a forum in Seoul to propose a new administrative reform strategy for the Vietnamese state amounted to more than just a bid for neighborly sympathy. The cross-cultural reproduction of the idea of an administrative elite might now have become global, but it had not lost the special regional resonances that it had had in east Asia centuries earlier when Vietnamese and Korean diplomats, meeting in Beijing, conducted "writing brush" conversations with each other in classical Chinese. Global thought was navigated more quickly if it came supplied with east Asian charts. It has been said that for continental European reformers in the 1700s, such as Voltaire, "Anglomania and sociology were practically synonymous."[18] It might be a considerable exaggeration to say that in China and Vietnam at the end of the twentieth century, the study of Japan or of South Korea was practically synonymous with sociology; global inspirations were too varied for that. But there were similarities between the way English institutions empowered the imaginations of some eighteenth-century continental European thinkers, in their search for liberty, and the ways Japanese and South Korean examples empowered Chinese and Vietnamese reformers now, in their pursuit of administrative rationality. Chinese and Vietnamese interest in what one Chinese writer in 1993 called "the east Asian pattern of the new replacing the old" did not necessarily imply any great love of Japan or South Korea, any more than eighteenth-century European thinkers' admiration for British institutions, and hopes of convergence with them, implied any love of the power of the British empire. (A poll of Beijing Chinese in 1994, asking what they thought about specific proposals for regional cooperation, revealed greater enthusiasm for the Association of Southeast Asian Nations—ASEAN—or for a big Asia-Pacific community in which purely east Asian interactions would be diluted, than it did for narrower east Asian notions of cooperation like a Sea of Japan economic zone or a Yellow Sea economic zone.)[19]

For the Vietnamese, in particular, a renewed interest in eastern Asian political theory came at a time, ironically, when Vietnam was being integrated into ASEAN (in 1995). And it required a huge effort to recover the basic linguistic resources for reentering the study of east Asian bureaucratic institutions. A 1997 survey of the cadres at nine Hanoi government ministries showed that 48 percent claimed to know English, as contrasted with a mere 12 percent who could still speak Russian and fewer than 3 percent who could speak Chinese. In proposing a plan in 1993 to make Chinese as well as English a strategic foreign language in Vietnamese cities and special economic zones, reformers at the Hanoi Foreign Language Teachers' College characteristically argued that learning Chinese would not just improve Vietnamese students' understanding of their own language (because "about 90 percent" of Vietnamese vocabulary had Chinese origins), but would make it easier for them to learn Japanese and Korean.[20]

New ventures in the shared east Asian exploration of administrative rationality began where the old ones had ended: with civil service examinations. The modern South Korean civil service examinations had been perfected and given a solid legal framework by the Park Chung Hee government (1961–1979). The new acceptance of bureaucracies, by the market Leninists in Beijing and Hanoi, stimulated an interest in them. These were not the old preindustrial Korean examinations, whose *yangban* officeholders the Japanese had pensioned off after making Korea their colony in

1910. As one Chinese admirer saw them in 1998, the new South Korean examinations were rather a commendable synthesis of Korea's precolonial
Confucian examinations, traceable back to eighth-century Silla; of the colonial Japanese standardization of the older Korean examinations traditions, which had made the examinations more efficient (while excluding
most Koreans from high government posts); and of postwar American influences in Korea, which introduced more relevant classifications of types
of bureaucratic posts.[21]

The irony of any Chinese admiration of the South Korean examinations
did not lie just in the Chinese use of South Korea as a source of state-
making inspirations, even if this did overthrow the familiar paradigm of
the Chinese tributary system of the past, by showing China learning from
Korea rather than the other way around. It also lay in the spectacle of a
contemporary east Asia, bent upon reinventing its own contribution to the
gestation of the modern, relying in part on the guidance of the one east
Asian country, Japan, that had never had such examinations in the preindustrial age. Nineteenth-century Japan, not having been a mandarinate,
thereby had a unique freedom to borrow its ideas from the homeland of
Max Weber: the Meiji Japanese civil service was modeled on that of Prussia. It had been extended to Korea when Ito Hirobumi became resident
general of the Japanese protectorate there. The modern South Korean bureaucracy was to a considerable degree not just a Japanese colonial creation, but a Japanese colonial creation that was based on Japanese understandings of European, especially German, civil service models.[22]

But for all their Japanese and German and American flavor, the new
South Korean examinations inevitably raised all the old questions, going
back centuries in China and Vietnam, about the hazards of text-based
meritocracy. Here was their continuity. One question familiar from the
past was: How much should the examinations be designed to encourage
social integration through a greater breadth of access to them, and how
much should they try to create a truly superior elite? A Chinese promoter
of the adoption of South Korean–type examinations in China in the 1990s
observed that the examinations' questions were "too difficult" to accommodate the standards of Chinese higher education, which were weaker
than South Korea's. If South Korean examinations were to be transferred to
China, they would have to be watered down for the masses of Chinese
party cadres, with little more than middle school educations, who might
need to be seduced into climbing a restored examinations-system ladder.

But Chinese observers praised the way the South Korean examinations gave preferential treatment to "model people" like soldiers or technologists who had given worthy service to the state.

Another question familiar from the past was: What weight should be given to test processes and writing-based knowledge, as opposed to face-to-face interviews and teachers' recommendations? Tang dynasty bureaucrats had fought over the answer to that one. But two features of the South Koreans' examinations made them seem irresistible to the Chinese or Vietnamese mandarins like Dao Tri Uc who were concerned to reject German fears of the Mannheim type about the administrative colonization of politics. One was the extent of their legal definition, compared with the meager "provisional" rules for such examinations in China and Vietnam, and the stability that resulted from it. The other was the South Korean examinations' emphasis upon "contemporary" subjects like information theory and computer-based forecasting and budgeting.[23] The new Vietnamese mandarinate, Dao Tri Uc had told South Koreans, would be one whose officials had a superior understanding of the "information sciences." Defining the "contemporary," in examination questions, as information theory and futurology gave the examinations a Saint-Simonian aura of postpolitical virtue. It was another way of saying: More mandarins and fewer old-fashioned cadres.

Science Worship and the Mandarin Ideal

These regional interpretations of the South Korean civil service examinations showed that any cross-cultural regeneration of the mandarin ideal in China and Vietnam was inextricably bound up with the political pretensions of science. Auguste Comte had prophesied in nineteenth-century Europe that scientists would ultimately displace priests and theologians in defining the moral foundations of the social order. In east Asia nearly two centuries later, it was much harder for scientists to displace new-style mandarins; on the contrary, the likelihood was that they would help the mandarins reestablish their supremacy.

Explaining the provisional regulations for state civil servants that were to take effect in China in 1993, the head of the Chinese personnel ministry stated that the object of rebuilding the civil service in China was the "science-ization" *(kexue hua)* of government organs' personnel management. It was unlikely that he saw this as a complete break with the ambitions of

Chinese history. In a similar vein, a Vietnam state airlines executive, writing in 1998, demanded that Vietnam do a better job of exploiting the "progressive" theories of management training from its precolonial past, as exemplified in the eighteenth-century Confucian philosopher Le Quy Don's views about talent; the executive told his readers in Hanoi and Ho Chi Minh City that Confucius himself was, in effect, the founder of global management studies, and that the American Frederick Winslow Taylor's theme that there was a "science" to the implementation of every form of work was simply a plausible industrial extension of preindustrial east Asian views of the human potential for achievement and its development.[24]

Science worship, as D. W. Y. Kwok explained it in 1965 in a pioneering work about scientism in Chinese thought, did not just mean the assumption that all aspects of the universe were knowable through the methods of science. It also meant the ideological tendency to use the respectability of science to promote policies in realms of action that might have had little obvious connection with science, as a scientist like Einstein would have understood it.[25] In the years after Kwok's book appeared, other scholars qualified it. They insisted, rightly, upon the existence of liberal scientists in China who had resolutely rejected and criticized all varieties of scientism, including the claims of Marxism to be a science, even if it was still true that for at least some Chinese and Vietnamese state intellectuals, science worship's totalistic search for a fundamental guide to truth of all kinds was hardly a dramatic change from the predispositions of preindustrial scholar-officials.[26]

In the absence of fully functioning democracies, however, science and technology were useful in helping members of the Chinese and Vietnamese elites, many of whom were engineers, to imagine states that embodied the common good, through their planning mystique if not through their voting processes. High technology and the information age were not diminishing the state in east Asia, despite the claims of some Western communications theorists that they would inevitably undermine power that operated hierarchically from the top down. On the contrary, with their science parks and visions of national "digital cities," high technology and the information age were serving as catalysts of state formation and of the state as an agency of a rational consciousness that could not be subverted by day-to-day political conflicts. Faith in the mediating power of science— a new answer to the mandarinates' old problem of who or what could mediate—ironically greatly exceeded actual government funding of science.

One Chinese scholar even calculated that at the end of the 1990s such multinational corporations as General Motors and Ford were each investing
more annually in research and development than was the entire Chinese
government. The erosion of the economic base of the Chinese and Vietnamese states, with the decline of revenues from provinces and state-
owned enterprises, contributed to this.[27] But an emerging stratum of state
intellectuals with specialized interests still needed scientistic fables of developmental optimism that could provide them with a voice, given the absence of any politically independent system of evaluation of intellectuals'
work such as overseas Chinese scientists like Zhenning Yang (Frank Yang)
had recommended to China in the early 1980s; and this need existed independently of government funding difficulties.

Nor were state intellectuals the only ones who liked scientistic fables of
development. Like Confucian family ideology in the past, these values
could be shared. In a 1996 Chinese poll, the members of the Chinese public who were asked expressed a far higher trust in science research organs
than in other Chinese state agencies, news organs, educational institutions,
or banks. The same survey showed that the Chinese public ranked highest
among the publics of fourteen countries polled in their support for science, but last among the fourteen publics in their basic understanding of
science; this perhaps confirmed the truism that a faith in science was most
likely to become a positive ideological force in societies where the actual
practices of scientific research were still limited.[28] Science popularizers in
China and Vietnam might complain that their publics did not have the capacity to distinguish between "real" and "false" science. But gullible people
in China in the 1990s who believed in prophets who could convert water
into oil, or in *qigong* masters' declarations that they could perform long-
distance miracles, were reflecting the same craving for scientistically con-
ceived hope in the future as could be found among the would-be mandarins in China's more than two hundred high-level management schools. A
poll of the "value orientations" of Shanghai party members in April 2000
found that fewer than half of them approved of the idea that doubt, or
skepticism, was the basic spirit of science.[29]

Of course east Asian scientism was also a distorted version of the Western variety. Perry Link, in the early 1990s, quoted a disgruntled Chinese
physics student as complaining that China's political leaders had little real
interest in science itself, just interest in the "face" or the "pride" that new
proton accelerators in China could give them.[30] But it would not have been

difficult to find Western politicians of the same stripe. In 2000 a Shanghai philosopher showed dismay at the crisis in "the sciences of thinking" in China, caused by the failure of general knowledge production to escape from the grip of the "hard" definitions of knowledge associated with the mechanistic attitudes of seventeenth-century and eighteenth-century physics.[31] But the conceptual habits of science worshippers lagged behind those of real scientists in the Western world too.

At the same time, scientism in China and Vietnam did have two notable features that were worth examining as part of the attempt to reinvent mandarin ideals there, cross-culturally or not. The first one was that Chinese and Vietnamese science worship had to legitimize the accommodation of an uglier imbalance of developmental risks between social classes than many Western theoreticians were inclined to acknowledge. The second one was that, incorporated as it was into the project of cross-cultural remandarinization, scientism in China and Vietnam inevitably aroused, if it did not fully revive, some of the critical reflexes associated with the old mandarinates.

As to the social imbalance of risks, it is not difficult to see why Anthony Giddens's Chinese translator should have rebuked him for his "Chernobyl is everywhere" view that modernity leveled the rich and the poor in their vulnerability to the hazards of history. The optimism of forms of science worship that pictured science as risk-free had a peculiar appeal in poor industrializing countries whose still huge agricultural economies had very little tolerance for the real risks of grassroots scientific experimentation, given the low incomes of their farmers, the dangers of tampering with nature, the absence of adequate technology extension services, the volatility of their markets for agricultural products, and the information distortions generated by the numerous intermediaries between the suppliers of agricultural technology and its recipients. Of the seven thousand or so high-technology research initiatives for agriculture produced on average each year by Chinese state scientists for Chinese farmers at the end of the twentieth century, only about one-third got converted into actual farming practices, about half the rate of conversion of test results into farming practices in European or North American agriculture.[32] The popularity of scientistic fables of development that obscured risks probably intensified in direct proportion to the hazards involved in the industrialization of real science innovations in the villages, and to the magnitude of class differences in the capacity to manage those risks. The diffusion of such elite fables downward worked to camouflage such class differences, perhaps in the same way that "how to get rich in the stock market" tracts camouflaged class differences in economic risk management for Western societies.

Under such circumstances, scientism could become as much ideological persuasion as administrative substance. Not for nothing did Vietnam's top sociologist of the 1980s call himself "Professor Future" (Tuong Lai), despite the fact that the Vietnamese state itself was doing relatively little science. (Of Vietnam's 1.2 million state officials in 1997, only about fifteen thousand worked in its science and industrial technology sector.)[33] Pictures of progress as a science-guaranteed adventure were part of the national eschatology. They circulated in east Asian science fiction, for example in the Chinese writer Ye Yonglie's celebrated story "The Man Who Flies to Pluto" of the late 1970s. (It imagined a Rip Van Winkle–like Tibetan serf who had been sleeping in a snowbank. When the serf in the story woke up and thawed out in the newly socialist Lhasa, he was so thrilled by modern China's achievements—such as a fully automated supermarket—that he agreed patriotically to have his body refrozen, so that he could participate in a Chinese exploration mission to Pluto.)[34]

As to the reappearance of old critical reflexes, one of the major ones in the old mandarinates was inside criticism of bureaucracies that endangered themselves through their own textual subjectivities. In the centuries when the Western world struggled to separate the spheres of church and state, east Asians had concerned themselves with the management of the equally hazardous relations between language and experience within at least nominally bureaucratic societies. The main nightmare was an alienation-producing government of circulating officials in which, as Sima Guang had put it in eleventh-century China, textual defamiliarizations of reality had become ingrained in bureaucratic life: the "written" had been made totally present and the "practical" or the "real" had become totally absent. Vietnamese thinkers had agreed. The "sickness" of the "mental operations" of an examinations-based polity could become so extreme, the Vietnamese literatus Ngo Thi Nham had warned in the 1700s, that students who took the examinations could no longer understand fully the principles of natural landscapes.[35]

At the end of the twentieth century elite subjectivity had again become a recognized problem for officials who served the postrevolutionary Chinese and Vietnamese states. As one Chinese sociologist observed in 1998, Chinese state intellectuals who researched Chinese villages now were not very good at understanding either the increasing politicization of village elites or the ways in which power in the villages was constructed from the bottom up; that was because they were far more concerned theoretically with how the state permeated village society from the top down, a neo-traditional attitude at odds with the spread of market-based commerce.[36] But the bureaucratic subjectivity problem was far more complex now, thanks to the inroads of linguistic globalization. More technocratic elites suffered the old anxieties about the written versus the real at a time when their very policy language was being imported from another civilization— a danger that a Sima Guang never imagined. An eminent Chinese economist pointed to the dangers for policymaking that might follow from the shallow comprehension and "mechanical copying" involved in the Chinese elite's wholesale acceptance, since 1978, of a flood of new foreign economic doctrines and their vocabularies (public choice theory, dual economic structure theory, modern corporation theory, scarcity theory, cost effectiveness theory, unbalanced growth theory).[37]

Neotraditional anxieties meant a return even of some of the actual metaphors of preindustrial political criticism. Among them there lurked a memory of the obsession with prebureaucratic "three dynasties" institutions, that is, with the salvationist vision of the ancient Xia, Shang, and Zhou dynasties, with their supposedly more perfect social arrangements, to which (as we saw earlier) Korean and Vietnamese idealists, as well as Chinese ones, had been devoted for many centuries. The positive function of this vision had been to provide mandarins with a theory of the social good, and with a sense of their social accountability in extra-bureaucratic terms. Its negative capacity had been to mythologize the desired future in such a text-bound way that the future became an intellectually closed domain whose definition was controlled almost entirely by bureaucratic elites.

One Chinese futurologist, writing in 1997, had this negative capacity in mind when he attacked what he called present-day China's Confucian futurology. Contemporary Chinese intellectuals, he argued, could not fully participate in international dialogues about global issues until they had purged themselves of their addiction to the mental habits of what this critic called their "three dynasties complex." According to the critic, the supposed mentality of a "three dynasties complex," or futurology without a future, was distorting the main bodies of managerial and scientific theory that China was importing from the West. It was doing so by molding such theories to narrow administrative ends, and, in the process, converting their open potentialities into closed mental constructs, in a manner not unlike that of the preindustrial "three dynasties" formula.

Here again was the fear that desirable forms of change could all too easily be converted into abstractions governed by their own vocabulary, the bureaucracy's written world displacing the world of open experience. The Chinese futurologist, in 1997, named six bodies of global theory as being particularly vulnerable, when they were imported into China, to being absorbed by the openness-foreclosing administrative interests of Chinese thinkers' alleged "three dynasties complex." They were information theory; dissipative structure theory; synergy theory; catastrophe theory; and, above all, control theory (cybernetics) and systems theory.[38]

The Mandarinization of Systems Theory

The mandarinization of systems theory and control theory, which overlap, and whose early prophets ranged from Ludwig von Bertalanffy to Norbert Wiener, is particularly notable. The former east Asian mandarinates undoubtedly offered fertile ground for them. The American mathematician and engineer Norbert Wiener, whose 1948 book on cybernetics was one of the foundational texts of the new theories, heralded the dawn of the age of computers as one in which it would be possible to adopt a holistic approach, based on simulated modeling, to understanding how the multiple elements of any physical or social system might interact with their environment, to stabilize or destabilize it.

The spirit of power implicit in the Chinese and Vietnamese reforms, and many of the reforms' more idealized techniques of power, are derived as much from Norbert Wiener's world as from Leninism or Confucianism or state capitalism. Wiener's world was that of the heavily militarized laboratory culture the English-speaking countries created in the 1940s and later to fight first Hitler and then the cold war. This laboratory culture was obsessed with "operations research" teams. (The first such team, composed of generals, mathematicians, physicists, and psychologists, was created in Britain in 1940 to plan the scientific side of the air war against Germany.) The systems theory that began to penetrate the English-speaking countries during and after World War Two vastly expanded the scope of the belief, associated with the earlier American engineer and management theorist Frederick Winslow Taylor, that individual human beings could overcome their biological and psychological limitations and be made to be more efficient—the highest virtue in this creed—through more rational organization based on the latest insights from the natural and social sciences. American management theory, with its implicit exaltation of the organization over the individual, coexists quite comfortably with the formulas for progress of the Asian Leninist reform states; and indeed the popularity of systems theory among the economists of the pre-1991 Soviet bloc suggests that the convergence has a long history. The term "system engineering"—which now litters the prose of Chinese and to a lesser degree Vietnamese reformers, and refers to the strategic planning and implementation of reforms—was probably first used decades ago by American business corporations like the Bell Telephone Company.

In the former mandarinates this new thought was at first more popular in wartime Hanoi, in the late 1960s and early 1970s, than in Mao Zedong's Beijing. Comprehensive mathematical models, one Hanoi cadre pointed out in 1973, could be made to yield a more optimistic view of Vietnam's future than the less mathematical, less holistic projections of less well educated cadres, especially during the bloody American war. And systems research could also be the antidote to the age-old problem in the mandarinates of the gap in understanding between administrators and administered. Theoretically, its computers could create reciprocal exchanges of information between "steering" agencies and the "objects" they steered. From 1968, when they were first imported, Soviet-made computers were used in north Vietnam by the railway service (to calculate the most efficient ways of repairing bombed bridges) and also by the hydraulics ministry (to research the effects of dike-management patterns on the Red River).[39]

By the late 1970s and early 1980s the Chinese elite were also thinking about organizational behavior in terms of postwar Western control theory and systems theory. Norbert Wiener had taught electrical engineering at Qinghua University in 1935–1936. Now he made a delayed but appropriately magnified impact. Qian Xuesen, the father of China's missile and space programs, published a book on system engineering in 1982; Yu Guangyuan and other elite reformers advanced the idea that all Chinese social and economic reforms after 1979 were a venture in system engineering; Chinese journals appeared with system engineering in their titles. Significantly, the first three administrative purposes to which this imported Western thought was applied in China were macroeconomic decisionmaking, the forecasting of oil field and gas field outputs, and population control.[40]

Information is the antithesis of uncertainty, the Hanoi scientist Phan Dinh Dieu told Vietnamese readers in 1973. But systems theory—a model of society disguised as a program for the circulation and consumption of information—is only as good as the information it gets. And its assumption that information is plentiful enough, and reliable enough, to permit scientific modeling of humans' interactions with their environments, marginalizes the precolonial mandarins' anxiety about the hazards of distorted or insufficient information. And their anxiety about such hazards— an anxiety without any real echoes in the Anglo-American laboratory culture of the 1940s—was one of their most interesting characteristics.

Here the indigenization of systems theory, and its awkward relationship with the precolonial mandarinates' fears about bureaucratic subjectivity, will be treated in connection with just one project. That is the coercive family planning programs of China and Vietnam at the end of the twentieth century. A book about "population system engineering," written by a Shanghai cybernetics expert, Wang Huanchen, inevitably appeared in China in 1985. It used computer-simulated analogues to establish "model relationships" between the Chinese population's changes in numbers and the Chinese economic surplus. This was in pursuit of a "scientific" idea of China's optimum rate of population growth. In March 2000 the communist party central committee and the state council reaffirmed, in a resolution about Chinese population control work, that planned reduction of the fertility rate was an exercise in system engineering. As a Qinghai province planner and demographer put it in a book about population control also published that year, Norbert Wiener had taught that society as a whole must be treated as an information system; the information sciences were the key that would reveal the internal relations, and even the laws, of population control.[41]

Nothing remotely comparable to the compulsory family planning programs of contemporary China and Vietnam was ever attempted under the preindustrial mandarinates. But it was true that the metaphorical representation of society as an "information system" both suited mandarin sensibilities and amounted to a potentially unprecedented extension of the old pattern of the administrative subjugation of the political, the written's subjugation of the real. And population control then threatened to become a far greater version of what tax reforms had been in eighth or eighteenth century east Asia: the place where bureaucratic rationality, simulated modeling or not, created unintended consequences in its attempts to reshape real human worlds.

By itself the gospel of population planning is not only indisputably modern but ideologically heterogeneous. At different times it has appealed to both liberal feminists and neofascist eugenicists. And Leninist Asia was not the only part of Asia that was to try compulsory family planning while proclaiming the human right of reproductive choice. After World War Two India was the first Asian country to try to implement planned, and sometimes coerced, reduction in fertility rates; Indonesia, under Suharto (1966–1998), also had a coercive population control program. But given their far longer histories of attempted bureaucracy, and the absence of postwar efforts at forced reduction of fertility rates in the European Leninist states (more worried about population losses after the destruction wrought by Hitler's war), the population control programs in China and Vietnam were one of the things for which east Asian Leninism would be long remembered. The managerial ambition that embraced decline in fertility rates as an inflexible norm of the modern did not just bureaucratize the political, as Mannheim had feared in 1929. It also bureaucratized the biological, in a revision or magnification of Mannheim's fears or prophecies such as he could never have imagined.

Inevitably, the Leninist population control programs in east Asia inspired rural rebellions, in some of which traditional folk beliefs in the coming of a messiah might mingle with opposition to birth control.[42] But the administrative compulsions behind Chinese and Vietnamese population planning theory were also vulnerable to what Tyrene White has called resistance from within the east Asian Leninist state's own ranks, given that population control applied in theory to everybody, not just villagers.[43] The dissatisfactions of state intellectuals, however muffled they seemed on this issue, offered one vantage point for examining how much any potential remandarinization project was likely to revive the reflexes of criticism displayed in mandarinates in the past.

It is an exaggeration, however understandable, to suggest that Malthusianism is the sole justification for autocratic family planning in China (or Vietnam); the genealogy of thought about family planning is more complex.[44] Malthus never went to China; Margaret Sanger (1879–1966) did; and Sanger, the American libertarian and birth control crusader, was the somewhat incongruous ancestor of the compulsory decline in the fertility rate that was later to be enforced by Leninist state bureaucracies. China's first society for research on birth control emerged in Suzhou in May 1922, just three months after Sanger's February 1922 speeches on Western birth-control theory, given in Beijing and Shanghai under the aegis of the leading Chinese liberal Cai Yuanpei, were rapturously heard and translated into Chinese. Sanger, under FBI surveillance when she went to China, had been a disciple of the anarchist Emma Goldman. For Sanger, as for Goldman, a woman's control over reproduction was as essential to revolutionary class struggle as workers' control over their conditions of employment. For Sanger, as for Goldman, contraception was the key to a "birth strike" that would reduce the supply of labor for greedy capitalist industrialists. Planned parenthood would end working-class servitude.[45]

But as early as 1930 the older habits of the Chinese managerial state, strengthened by imports of the multiplying Western doctrines of technocratic rationality, began to swallow up Margaret Sanger's ideal of liberation. In 1930 Chen Changheng (1888–1937) published a book devoted to the connection between "the ideology of the three people's principles" and government population policy. Chen's book proposed that the state make fertility control and delayed marriages one of its management tasks, based upon the state's own investigations of how big a population was "rational." Chen had further suggested in 1935 that the state-defined standards of ideal population size would have to encompass the perceived needs of economics, national defense, politics, society, education, culture, eugenics, and medicine.[46] So the illusion that a workable theory of population control, based on so many different variables, not only was possible but could be enforced by the government from the top down, existed in eastern Asia before the invention of cybernetics and systems theory in the West in the late 1940s and the migration of this new managerial thought to China and Vietnam from the end of the 1970s.

The new managerial thought, however, magnified the presumption. It led to a coercive policy of one child (or two) per family, in which the Chinese state imposed (as of 1995) on the local governments below it no fewer than five different kinds of annual population targets. These ranged from desired numbers of newborns to quotas for total population size per jurisdiction for the end of each year. Such targets were based not on real numbers, but on numbers predicted in advance. The calculations of the state leadership cadres who formulated them were unnaturally inflexible—so one disgruntled member of a national family planning commission charged in 1995—precisely because such cadres were remote from the real contingencies of population theory's application.[47] Such a willful bureaucratization of the future was presumably what was meant by the criticism that Chinese state thinkers suffered from a "three dynasties complex" with respect to systems theory: a tendency inherited from Chinese bureaucratic history by which they turned the future into a closed and controlled administrative space.

Yet some of the roots of this new "three dynasties complex" were Western as well as Chinese. After World War Two, Western demographers became, in Philip Hauser's memorable word, "schizophrenic." But we have met a milder form of this "schizophrenia" before: among preindustrial east Asian mandarins who analyzed policy issues both normatively and empirically without considering themselves to be schizophrenic in so doing.

The "schizophrenia" of post-1945 Western demographers allegedly lay in their unprecedented "confusion" as to whether they should be empirical scientists or social engineers. By the 1940s the Western world had accumulated a large literature about the nature of fertility decline in western Europe and North America. This literature was descriptive and analytical, not normative. It promoted historical understanding, not managed change. Beginning in the late 1940s, however, the notion of fertility decline during industrialization escaped from its historical describers. Western demographers came to see it, not as something that needed to be explained in the West, but as something that needed to be induced in the non-West. The rise of "demographic transition theory" in the 1940s was crucial to this development. Western demographers used it to universalize, and idealize, the history of Western fertility rates. They proposed that all the national populations on the planet could be placed on a single continuum of demographic development that had (as usual) three stages.[48] Wallerstein's definition of the classical ideology of modernity—the faith that improved technology and expanded human liberation were "symbiotic" objectives that could not possibly contradict each other—now heavily infected the Western languages of science worship before they were transposed to east Asia.

In east Asia, however, regional materials could be used to consolidate "demographic transition theory" in bureaucratic minds, as part of the broader conversion of systems theory into a closed structure of norms. Famous Japanese demographers such as Kuroda Toshio had proposed that east Asians might undergo a common demographic transition, with each east Asian society occupying a different rung of the temporal ladder. Japan, in this scheme, began its "ultimate" or "final" transition to low fertility rates in 1947; Hong Kong and Singapore began theirs in 1961 and 1964 respectively; and China supposedly began its "final" transition to low fertility rates in the last years of Mao. Kuroda called this scheme his "diffusion theory" of demographic transition.

By the 1990s, in some Chinese hands, Kuroda Toshio had metamorphosed from a demographer into a useful prophet of a future east Asian solidarity in which the state coercion of human reproductive behavior in some parts of the region could be overlooked. In reinterpretations of Kuroda's "diffusion," the shared east Asian classical culture and its values, when combined with self-interested Japanese and South Korean capital investment in other east Asian countries with more abundant labor supplies, would guarantee economic growth and a final demographic transition for all east Asians, giving them all biological modernity.[49] In this demographic "end of history" scenario, forced abortions disappeared. Fertility decline was no longer seen as politically imposed, but as an historical inevitability. This type of sublimation was a mandarinal one, even if the notion of such a demographic transition itself, as the foundation of modernity, only went back to the 1940s and was originally intended to be specific to the West.

Much Chinese reformist thought circulated in Vietnam; Vietnamese cadres could even read translations of Chinese books that anthologized Deng Xiaoping's ideas about such things as the uses of "people of talent."[50] But at first glance the demographic crisis in Vietnam, with which reviving mandarin values might be seen to interact, differed considerably from the one in China, as did Vietnam's state family planning programs. There were at least one million Vietnamese war deaths between 1965 and 1975, possibly many more. Proportionately, this catastrophe was surely comparable to that of the eight million men killed in all of Europe in World War One. Indeed it helped to produce Vietnamese politburo leaders after 1975 who were fatally similar to the grey, tired politicians who governed much of Europe in the 1920s. In contrast to China, Vietnam suffered from a shortage of men, not of women, because of the war and also because of the greater emigration of men after 1975 to avoid conscription. Coercive birth control in Vietnam was less severe than China's, and also less successful.

A Vietnamese state policy of one or two children per family, sketched out in Hanoi as early as 1963, did not effectively materialize until 1988, nine years after the similar initiative in China. It did not require as much intrusive monitoring of women's pregnancy statuses; and it was more open to outside advice and assistance, which came variously from the United Nations, from Australia, and even from nongovernmental population and development organizations in Thailand, Vietnam's neighbor and former adversary. Vietnamese provincial planning brochures, as Daniel Goodkind has shown, even tried to teach birth control by means of soothing songs, with titles like "Hope you are like a one-child woman." Such songs implied that men would long for women who were not "thin and faded" from too much childbearing.[51]

Yet the Vietnamese managerial state, although weaker and less experienced than the one in China, still looked broadly similar to China's in its approach to population "system engineering" from above. Upward and downward mobility for its local cadres depended to some extent upon their performance in implementing national policies regarding fertility rates. There was the same ideological use of scientist language to reconcile what Wallerstein held to be the two incompatible narratives of modernity—the narrative of an increase in human emancipation and the narrative of an increase in technological control over nature—in such a way as to conceal the coercion in Vietnamese state population programs.

The Reemergence of Hazard Analysis

The bureaucratization of biology was imposed by state hierarchies from the top down, with the center giving population planning quotas to the provinces and the provinces giving them to prefectures and counties. The manner, if not the purpose, of this enterprise would not have seemed totally unfamiliar to eighth-century Chinese tax reformers of the Yang Yan kind. Historians writing in the twenty-third century might well see Chinese and Vietnamese history at the end of the twentieth century as a period in which post-1800 Western organization theory—which tried to remove the politics from supposedly purely technical appreciations of organizational problems—merged with much older, embryonically modern east Asian bureaucratic traditions that had recurrently, in their critics' eyes, displaced experience with texts. The hazard was that policymaking lapses into subjectivity could now be doubly determined, both by the local inapplicability of global theory and by the self-isolation of domestic bureaucratic practice. Not surprisingly, Chinese and Vietnamese criticisms of this hazard sometimes also had a neotraditional flavor.

Some of the criticisms addressed the ancient question of nonconfrontational alienation caused by the gap between the state's ambitions and the wishes of its people. One of China's most eminent state population planning specialists, Zha Ruichuan (1925–2001), told a Beijing conference on fertility decline in 1995 that he feared the global policymaking sciences' overproduction of theories, some of which were disguised recyclings of older theories. The effect of the surplus production of theories was to create a rhetorical "tide" upon which Chinese elites were likely to drift, away from any consciousness of local realities. The bureaucratic imbalance between knowledge and action would become so great as to make local Chinese needs invisible.

More specifically, Zha characterized voluntary reduction in fertility rates as "objective." Coerced reduction in fertility rates, in contrast, was "subjective." "Subjective" decline in fertility rates was likely to run far greater risks than its "objective" counterpart. In addition to the risks that fertility decline encounters everywhere (aging of the population, falling consumer demand, inadequate labor supplies, loss of social vitality), "subjective" decline would also create a concealed divorce between administrators and administered. Symptoms of the divorce would include, among others, the growing unreliability of the population statistics provided from below.[52] At least part of this theme of the deadly trap of state "subjectivity" and local noncompliance certainly echoed the equivalent concerns, in very different contexts, of centuries of Chinese bureaucratic critics.

Another way in which the mandarins of the past had audited their own bureaucracy's rationality had been to suggest that its policymakers were asking the wrong questions, about such issues as the causes of poverty. The population planning debate also provoked the resurrection of this critical habit from the old mandarinates. Dipping into systems theory's seemingly bottomless supply of engineering metaphors, a number of Chinese policy intellectuals in the 1980s had become preoccupied with defining what they called China's "rational population load-bearing capacity" *(heli renkou chengzai liang)*, treating their society as if it were a giant artificial container. They could not agree on what the optimum capacity for the container might be: their projections ranged from 700 million to 1.6 billion people. But their search for a paradigm of administrative certainty in intrinsically uncertain circumstances, hardly a new tendency, was challenged.

One critic in Shanghai pointed out that it was not at all clear that China's environmental crisis was the result of too much population pressure. Rather, it might be the outcome of massively wasteful consumption patterns and excessively low state efficiency in the use of natural resources. Japan's far more efficient energy consumption, in particular, was said to expose both the backwardness of Chinese state planners and managers and China's "chronic disease" of violating public resources because the state's fragmented structure prevented any one authority from taking full responsibility for them.[53] Japan, in fact, had contradictory functions in the self-understanding of the postcollectivist Asian Leninist states. On the one hand, Japan was the centerpiece of a narrative of the convergence of regional fertility rates that allowed officials to obscure the much more authoritarian manner of the Chinese reduction of population growth, allowing the Chinese state to develop a more rational self-image than it was entitled to claim, even at the cost of estrangement from its own public. But Japan was also the external example that could be used, by inside critics, to illuminate the unreality of this self-image and the absence of enough practical empiricism as a restraint on the behavior of the theory-making elite.

Some critics of the population control bureaucracies did not just echo critical strategies that had been used in the past; they directly accused the population planners of reproducing specific forms of bureaucratic subjectivity that had flourished in the preindustrial period. As one example, in 1990 a famous Vietnamese specialist on south Vietnam's regional culture alleged that Hanoi's campaign to reduce fertility in the Mekong delta had failed because of its reliance on the neotraditional presumption that the delta's people, like those of the rest of Vietnam, were governed by a faith in Confucianism, Taoism, and Buddhism. This, however, was simply a continuation of preindustrial classificatory schemes and elite misunderstandings of popular values from previous centuries. The people of the southwest delta, far from being loyal to the old dynastically sanctioned "three religions," were vegetarian pantheists with a strong taboo against the taking of life. As such they were contemptuous both of state family planners and of old-fashioned female abortion specialists; they could not be influenced by remote bureaucratic stereotypes of what they were supposed to believe.[54]

Proposed cures for the problem of bureaucratic subjectivity in Chinese and Vietnamese population management programs also had a familiar ring, in Vietnam as well as in China. In Vietnam in particular, the state's coercive family planning crusade, like the state itself, had had relatively little success among the hill-country minorities. (The number of Hmong people in northern Vietnam more than doubled between 1960 and 1989, and the women of at least six recognized ethnicities in Vietnam in the late 1980s were producing on average eight children.) The solution, one expert wrote, was for the government to rescue itself by disregarding its own leadership structures and seeking the help of the natural leaders of minority society, the "people with prestige" in their lineages and villages.[55] In practice such advice would not have been easy to follow. It meant negotiating with polygamous Bahnar elders reluctant to sanction limits on their numbers of wives or children; Hmong patrilineages needing many sons to enhance their authority; and even (among the ethnic Vietnamese) Catholic village heads deploring birth control devices as an attack on their religion. But it would also not have been original. Centuries of county magistrates in east Asia had understood instinctively what one of them, Wang Huizu, expounded so memorably at the end of the 1700s. That was the necessity of resolving the estrangement that bureaucratic states generated in local communities, by informally or surreptitiously recruiting the unofficial intermediaries (teenaged informants with a command of "country talk," in Wang's scheme) that such communities created by themselves.

At the end of his book about the "third revolution"—the emergence of postfeudal professional elites in the modern world—Harold Perkin suggested that such elites were likely to abuse their power. He implied pessimistically that we might not even want to solve the problem of how to prevent this. His position was that this was a problem for the present and the future in the West; but despite the fact that mandarins were not entirely like the professionals he had in mind, this was also part of a long, continuing crisis in east Asia. In east Asia, however, the emergence of such elites had been invested with optimism as well as pessimism. The spirit of hope also continued. The Chinese cultural nationalist and institutional economist Sheng Hong, writing in a society with a deeper tradition of anxiety about postfeudal elites, could still observe in 1993 that he could perfectly well imagine an ideal political structure that integrated democracy with government by an administratively skilled moral elite. In such a scheme the elite would claim a new function, as the "virtual agents" of two constituencies who could never vote: human beings who had not yet been born, and nonhuman living creatures. The new mandarin elite's legitimacy as "virtual agents" of the human future, and of nonhuman nature, would be derived from its members' privileged historical understanding of the value of self-restraint. Only people who practiced self-restraint, in order to help others, would be worthy of being called an elite.[56]

Such an elite would, of course, have less in common with the ideas of

Norbert Wiener than with those of the Song dynasty scholar-official Fan Zhongyan (989–1052), famous for his belief that the ideal public servant should be first in worrying about the world's troubles and last in enjoying its pleasures. The elite policymaker who, through superior moral consciousness, could bear the burdens of others and restrain his own appetites was probably as important an ideal in medieval east Asia as the totally chivalrous knight was in European history at the time Fan Zhongyan lived, if far more of a postfeudal creation. Whether such an elite could ever come close to existing in the twenty-first century was almost beside the point. Its ghostly presence in contemporary east Asian thought showed how important the consolations of a mandarin approach to politics still were, despite the hazards.

Conclusion

Western political empires, in Asia and elsewhere, were decolonized after 1945. But the Western knowledge empire, which once accompanied the political empires, remains largely intact. It now globalizes what has been most innovative in Western thought in the past century. And postcolonial Asians have little trouble recognizing that this is management theory, not theory about liberal democracy, even if Western universities' philosophy departments continue to remain in the dark about the point. In terms of global influence, if not of quality of thought, F. W. Taylor, Henri Fayol, Norbert Wiener, Herbert Simon, and even Alvin Toffler and Lee Iacocca, outdistance Karl Popper or John Rawls or Isaiah Berlin.

In the former Asian mandarinates the trend has been so clear that in 1991 Do Muoi, the general secretary of the Vietnamese Communist Party, publicly argued that political reform required a clear division among the legislative, executive, and judicial branches of the Vietnamese state, not because this would facilitate democracy, but because it would better enable Vietnam to borrow "global achievements" in the "state organization and management sciences."[1] Even the ghosts of Western thinkers whose theories about human improvement were intended to be unequivocally liberating, such as Margaret Sanger, have been absorbed by state population-control bureaucracies (in China, an army of 180,000 full-time personnel at the county or subcounty level by 1990) whose purpose has been the managed standardization of their societies' "child-bearing cultures." Indeed, even nineteenth-century Western fictional heroes who embodied a heroic liberating (or problem-solving) individualism have been reincarnated in Sinicized form in post-1978 China as servants of the managerial state. For example, writers working for the Beijing ministry of public security have been paid to invent Chinese detectives modeled upon Sherlock Holmes; the Chinese fictional versions of Holmes are communist cadres who supposedly demonstrate the "prowess" of the state ministry for which they toil.[2]

Economic globalization has "ignited" a worldwide competition for "people of talent," the Chinese army newspaper observed in 2000.[3] Successful Western business corporations from Silicon Valley to Wall Street are being converted into external reference points for validating—in present-day capitalist terms—the embryonically modern struggle of centuries of post-aristocratic Asian mandarins to win types of respect for themselves that were connected more to administrative merit than to fully hereditary statuses. We have very few means yet of imagining just where the shadowy confluence or even synthesis of these two traditions will lead. But if such confluences or syntheses are an emerging feature of political theory in the former mandarinates, what has their past political theory been?

Post-1945 Western scholarship has recognized historical east Asian achievements in science and education, and more recently (in the work of writers mentioned earlier in this text) in the economic life and the state framework of precapitalist China at least. But the past political theory of China and the other two mandarinates has not been so easily accommodated. It has seemed dangerous to see this political theory as having any connection with contemporary concerns, and not just because of exaggerated "linguistic contextualist" fears that the linguistic meanings, authorial intentions, and historical contexts of this theory have been rendered irretrievable by the drastic interventions of imperialism and revolution. Yet historians have explored the variety of the political languages of preindustrial Europe, and their contested nature, even in the most absolutist monarchies. The failure at least to try to do the equivalent for eastern Asian political theory leads to a sort of Orientalism by the back door, an indirect confirmation of Asian stasis. Surely it is time to take the political and administrative theory of the three mandarinates more seriously, not just treating it as an adjunct of something we call "Confucianism," or as an intellectual reflection of a political typology we call "feudalism."

This will not be easy. A brilliant scholar of Korea has recently argued that the Korea we know now very recently "emerged from one of the most class-divided and stratified societies on the face of the earth, almost caste-like in its hereditary hierarchy."[4] Class stratification and genuinely feudal castes are not the same thing, however: and the world of Korean thought whose existence is implied by this generalization desperately needs to be put in comparative terms. One has only to compare Korean thinkers of the 1600s and 1700s with their European counterparts to detect what was significantly missing from Korean "feudalism." That was the political language by which essentially feudal forms of political power were comprehensively mystified for the public eye.

Take, for example, the French jurist Charles Loyseau (1564–1627), whose treatise on the French political and social order retained its influence until the French Revolution. Loyseau compared the subdivisions of the French class structure to celestial hierarchies; portrayed princes as "living images of God"; described one form of French nobility as exceeding human memory in its origins; and lovingly detailed the nobility's existing status-defining varieties of coats of arms, spurs and gilded harnesses, and gold chains. That was feudal thought. And even after the French Revolution broke out, a British thinker like Edmund Burke (1729–1797) could still argue that bad monarchies deserved respect, because they were interwoven by sheer length of historical habit with things more valuable than themselves. In Korea by this time, in contrast, examinations and bureaucracy had slowly and invisibly eroded the resources of any genuinely feudal language of politics of this still vital European kind.

Indeed when one Korean Confucian reformer, Chong Yagyong (1762–1836), analyzed Korean kings, he argued that they were no more than lead dancers in a troupe of dancers, and that if incompetent they should be bloodlessly removed. Chong's language with respect to the monarchy was a language of pure administrative utility. Equally telling was Chong's unwillingness or inability to locate the upper-class magnates who he presumed would remove bad kings in any persuasively imagined ancient context of law, custom, religion, happiness, and "honor," as his British contemporary Burke might have done. Chong was not a typical Korean scholar-official, of course; he was an ambitious reformer and critic of the state orthodoxy's metaphysics. But it may still be hypothesized that he, and his fellow Chinese and Vietnamese mandarins, could summon up no more than the fragments of a real "feudal" outlook, compared to the European thinkers of the same period who wished to do so.[5]

Moreover, many of the issues treated by mandarin thought had little to do with any conceivable ideas of feudalism, or for that matter directly with Confucianism. They are, however, issues of continuing relevance to us. Two of them deserve restatement here. One was the problem of the self-subversion of formally nonhereditary, merit-testing monocultures. The more pessimistic Chinese thinkers suggested that the long-term trends in China's great experiment with meritocracy had included an inflation in the numbers of people thought to be talented; a standardizing oversimplification of the sources from which merit might be thought to be generated, or in which it might be found; a growing indifference to the question of how talent might be specifically used; and a growing substitution of linguistic and textual authority for actual experience.

Thinkers in the other two mandarinates inevitably emphasized such anxieties differently. Vietnamese analysts of the same problem, for example, hardly worried about the numerical inflation of the meritocracy; their struggle just to create a critical mass of "talent" in Vietnam was too great. But they shared the sense that the effort to rule through "talent" produced a series of interesting crises in the legitimization of its definitions. They also shared Chinese concerns about the relationship between visible and invisible power, especially the treacherous invisibility-creating mechanisms of language. As for Korean analysts, the complaints of officials like Yu Suwon—about the forms of argumentation within the Korean government in the 1700s becoming a device for corrupting thought and disguising indefensible forms of subjectivity—were probably not equaled in the English-speaking world, for sheer vehemence at least, until George Orwell began to attack the politics of language in twentieth-century dictatorships.

A second issue was the problem of bureaucratic accountability. This was the "bureaucratic accountability paradox" as it has come to be known, with significant belatedness, in post–World War Two Western public administration theory. Mandarins, as nonhereditary public servants who circulated from one position to another, might become more concerned about their next career moves than about the public good, as Sima Guang argued so memorably in eleventh-century China. Their self-esteem no longer came from inner satisfaction at successfully embodying aristocratic virtues. Even the supposedly transcendental ruler they served might be deflatingly characterized (as by Gu Yanwu in seventeenth-century China) as no more than the "so-called Son of Heaven."[6] Outside demands for performance-based accountability that were too rigidly or demeaningly codified to compensate for this might backfire, by eroding what moral self-possession remained to them, undermining their capacity to satisfy such demands.

Only by fully appreciating the problem of bureaucratic accountability is it possible to recognize the magnitude of the achievement of what we call "Confucianism" in the mandarinates. Of course Confucian teachings shaped the educational milieu from which Chinese, Korean, and Vietnamese administrators were drawn. And even if the Confucian-flavored ideologies of these three public administrations rarely reflected what such administrations actually did, there was still a need for idealized versions of what they ought to do to justify their existence, to checkmate rivals (such as military leaders), and to strengthen the relative authority of higher officials over lesser ones. But beyond that, the great achievement of Confucianism was to prevent the problem of bureaucratic accountability from becoming extreme.

Confucian teachings achieved this despite the fact that Confucianism was originally a prebureaucratic creed, reflecting feudal forms of hereditary power, and lacking even much consciousness, among its founders at least, of a money economy. The three mandarinates could be described as a great experimental ground for trying to make prebureaucratic ethics nourish what were often increasingly insufficient types of bureaucratic self-esteem. As such, they narrowly anticipated the even greater problem of how modern human beings can maintain a sense of right and wrong if they preserve only the remnants of premodern religious beliefs in personal immortality. "Gentlemen," the Vietnamese scholar-official Le Quy Don wrote in 1773, ought to be capable of reading the auguries correctly when they founded states, of giving the proper orders on hunting trips, of writing the proper poems on hilltops, of haranguing soldiers properly in war, of choosing the proper posthumous honorary titles for dead people, and of making the proper prayers on sacrificial occasions.[7] This entirely archaic definition of the mandarin ideal significantly treated mandarins as warriors and priests and royal surrogates, rather than as obedient paper-pushing officials. Of course it corresponded to no actual Vietnamese administrator of the 1700s. But that was the point. A feudal text like the one we associate with the philosopher Mencius, who died in the third century B.C.E. if he existed, took for granted the existence of a warrior aristocracy, yet became progressively more influential in the next two thousand years as China and the other mandarinates less and less resembled the society the author or authors of the text would have known.

If meritocracies did not lead to civil war, as Pascal had predicted, incomplete ones could provoke a consciousness of relative deprivation. Aware of this, the Chinese scholar and palace tutor Hu Xu (d. 1736) lamented that all China's schools in the 1700s reached no more than two or three percent of the people, leaving in limbo whole categories of farmers, gardeners, artisans, merchants, woodcutters, fishermen, and peddlers. Affirmative action was the solution for him as it has become more recently for us: Hu proposed the expansion of meritocracy in moral terms, through the official entitlement of the "filial sons" and "devoted brothers" among such uneducated commoners, and the conferring of privileges upon them comparable to those enjoyed by junior mandarin aspirants already inside the examinations-and-promotions machine. But the problem with such a remedy was that it would have undermined the scarcity value of the status attributes of the existing mandarins, calling into question as it did so the reduced pseudo-aristocratic resources of the imaginary world that stood between them and corruption.[8]

Some of the losers—the excluded—mimicked or subverted from below the meritocratic forms that had marginalized them. The ultimate revenge of the excluded came when the leader of the Taiping rebellion in nineteenth-century China, himself a failed examination candidate, set up his own examinations and allowed most of their applicants to pass. Among a whole gender of the excluded, few Chinese elite women may have behaved like the erudite bride in Wu Jingzi's eighteenth-century satire about scholars, who set essay topics for her new husband on their honeymoon; but the presence of vengeful female ghosts in the recorded nightmares of male examination candidates hints at the latent gender defensiveness of would-be mandarins in a society without final answers about how inclusive meritocracy should be. For some mandarins, such as Chen Hongmou, the misbehaving government clerks who were also excluded from the formal meritocracy evoked more than mere defensiveness. Like modern Western intellectuals who feel that what is wrong with the Enlightenment Project is that it has never been fully tried, men like Chen saw the clerks as a symptom of the tragic incompleteness of the meritocratic venture.

These concerns were part of a past with unmistakable echoes in the present, because of their incipiently modern features as well as because of the unresolved issues of present-day Chinese and Vietnamese (and North Korean) politics. At first glance, for example, the People's Republic of China hardly resembles the various political versions of imperial China that came and went in the two millennia before 1911. Five levels of government have replaced the three levels that existed between the thirteenth and the nineteenth centuries; far more government personnel, in percentage terms as well as in numbers, are concentrated at the local county and township levels than would have been true before 1911; the township functionaries who have, to some extent, replaced the imperial county clerks, are better educated (many of them being schoolteachers); and the postimperial party state itself is attempting to carry out an unprecedented industrial revolution, with all the obvious consequences of environmental pollution and rising popular expectations. Yet the village tax reforms that began in Anhui province and spread more generally through China in the early twenty-first century reminded Chinese observers themselves of nothing so much as imperial China's clerks problem, or the chronic inability of a postfeudal Chinese state to mobilize subordinate state agents, outside the center's ambit, for central government goals.

As one tax reform specialist at the Beijing state council put it in 2004, the tax reforms would do no good unless they smashed "the Huang Zongxi law." Huang Zongxi (1610–1695) was a seventeenth-century mandarin of enormous critical power. His angry "law" was that imperial China's cycles of tax reforms had all failed in the same way: they had always increased the level of exploitation of the common people without ever decreasing it and returning China to a Mencian golden age of low tax rates. In communist-ruled China the "law" took the form of counterproductive resistance by local functionaries to top-down tax reductions, through the surreptitious replacement of taxes by unauthorized fees. This politically contrapuntal behavior would have been instantly recognizable to any pre-1911 mandarin. Indeed the Chinese township functionaries whom Chinese state council reformers now attack could respond in exactly the same way that Chong Yagyong suggested Korean petty officials should respond, two centuries ago, to their higher bureaucratic critics: by asking the higher officials what their own relationship was to the common people, that they could claim the right to control and punish petty officials on the common people's behalf.[9]

In a rapidly industrializing China run by engineers, not old-fashioned mandarins, is tax reform still little more than a footnote to the tax reform history of imperial China? All that can be said here is that the postcolonial state suffers from the same problems of bureaucratic subjectivity and vertical coordination as its postfeudal predecessors. But the atmosphere now is one of science worship in which the preindustrial mandarins' interest in moral rationality as well as the administrative variety ("inner sageliness" as the precondition for "outer kingliness") has almost disappeared. The result is that tax reformers have to borrow their consciousness of the hazards of tax reform, and thus the critical standards for their own administrative behavior, from a seventeenth-century mandarin like Huang Zongxi. Yet Huang himself had to borrow the critical standards for his "law" from a much earlier, far more feudal Chinese history, invoking "three dynasties" ideals to escape from his own bureaucratic present. The hazard of bureaucratic procedures whose legal resources are more up to date than their historical moral resources is an old problem in east Asia. But it is no longer found only there.

Bureaucracy, of course, never seemed irreversible or inevitable to most east Asians in the preindustrial age, unlike our probable view of it now. These states were, as has been said before, precarious syntheses of bureaucratic and nonbureaucratic elements. In the two thousand years between its first unification as an empire and the Opium War, China enjoyed any real semblance of bureaucratic unity for barely half the time. The quasi-aristocratic privileges and social aloofness of Choson Korea's *yangban* elite obscured, if they did not always frustrate, the revolutionary nature of Korea's civil service examinations in world history. And the great meltdown of bureaucratic rule in Vietnam between 1500 and 1800—to the point where the north, in 1777, had barely ten percent of the numbers of civil and military officials the entire kingdom had had three centuries earlier, if Le Quy Don's calculations are to be believed—showed how fragile the mandarinate project was there. But even this meltdown was viewed by Le Quy Don in a spirit of administrative utility, not of outraged feudal prescriptiveness; Le Quy Don said that the meltdown had been a good thing, because the costs of the bureaucratic model imported from Ming China had outstripped the Vietnamese capacity to pay for them.[10]

And yet, if examinations-based meritocracy did not seem to be an irresistible trend for most preindustrial east Asians, any more than democracy seemed so in the West in the two millennia after Athens lost the Peloponnesian War, there was still always an inkling that the clock could not really be turned back for good, that the need to define talent in postfeudal ways was too important a principle ever to be forgotten. Jiao Xun (1763–1820), the brilliant Qing dynasty classicist, poured scorn on Gu Yanwu's idea that the way to solve the Chinese solidarity deficit was to make some government positions, like county magistrates, hereditary again; even this halfway house would be bound to collapse in a society where the instincts of meritocracy had become dominant.[11] East Asian mandarins worried about the ways in which administrative language, not anchored to feudal power structures that stretched to the bottom of society, might distort local needs and experiences. But as the Vietnamese mandarin Phan Huy Chu pointed out in the early 1800s, a bureaucracy also meant rules, or normative standards, for such activities as tax collecting, which monarchs could not "avoid" and which ensured political predictability—a form of freedom from too much contingency.[12]

In a patronizing 1922 book, *The Problem of China*, the British philosopher Bertrand Russell depicted China as an economically and socially backward "artist nation" that would have to modernize rather than "remain an interesting survival of a bygone age, like Oxford University or the Yellowstone Park."[13] Yet at the time when Russell, an aristocrat himself, wrote these words, the Britain to which he belonged still had a hereditary House of Lords, and an aristocratic principle that would have seemed outdated in China even one thousand years earlier, when the Chinese embarked upon their great experiment of recruiting their ruling "worthies" through civil service examinations rather than just through hereditary social claims.

What his Chinese translator wrote about Anthony Giddens—that Giddens both underestimated the ancientness of the risks of modernity and wrongly posited a single source of global modernity in seventeenth-century Europe—must be enlarged. The modern, comprehensively understood, surely has multiple sources, in the east Asian mandarinates as well as elsewhere. But the multiple sources are not necessarily important in themselves. They gain importance only in connection with Walter Benjamin's famous 1940 warning that a "state of emergency" is the rule in human history, not the exception, or with William McNeill's insistence that modernity means power but also vulnerability, the undiminished "conservation of catastrophe."[14] East Asian traditions of the political uses of human reason, and the theorizations of risks associated with those uses, are well worth studying in their own right, by anyone who lives on the side of a volcano, as we all do. And a fuller recovery of the multiple sources of the modern that have been lost will only make the West's invention of steam engines and stock markets more, not less, historically fascinating.

Notes

Index

Notes

Introduction

1. Larry Siedentop, *Tocqueville* (Oxford: Oxford University Press, 1994), 83–84; Rupert Wilkinson, *The Prefects: British Leadership and the Public School Tradition* (Oxford: Oxford University Press, 1964), 127.
2. E. R. Curtius, *European Literature and the Latin Middle Ages* (London: Routledge and Kegan Paul, 1953), trans. W. R. Trask, 254.
3. Bruno Latour, *We Have Never Been Modern* (London: Pearson Education, 1993), trans. Catherine Porter, 41, 46–47, 120–121.
4. Harold J. Berman, *Law and Revolution: The Formation of the Western Legal Tradition* (Cambridge, Mass.: Harvard University Press, 1983), 538–558.
5. Yan Jiaqi, *Quanli yu Zhenli* (Power and truth), (Beijing: Guangming ribao chubanshe, 1987), 82–90.
6. Ding Shouhe, comp., *Zhongguo lidai zhiguo ce xuancui* (Selected highlights of Chinese state administration policies through the centuries), (Beijing: Gaodeng jiaoyu chubanshe, 1994), 664–667.
7. Li Fu, "Zongzi zhuji yi" (On the leader of the patrilineal kinship line as master of sacrifices), in He Changling, comp., *Huangchao jingshi wenbian* (A compilation of statecraft essays of the present court), (Taibei: Wenhai, 1972 ed.), 66: 7–7b. The term "aristogenic" is in Timothy Brook, "Family Continuity and Cultural Hegemony: The Gentry of Ningbo," in J. Esherick and M. Rankin, eds., *Chinese Local Elites and Patterns of Dominance* (Berkeley: University of California Press, 1990), 27–50.
8. Yi Ik, in Peter H. Lee, ed., *Sourcebook of Korean Civilization* (New York: Columbia University Press, 1996), 15–21.
9. *Da Qing Gaozong Chunhuangdi shilu* (Veritable records of the Qing Qianlong reign), (Tokyo: Okura shuppan kabushiki kaisha, 1937–1938), 1088: 3–6; Charles Ingrao, *The Habsburg Monarchy 1618–1815* (Cambridge: Cambridge University Press, 1994), 155.
10. Noam Chomsky, *American Power and the New Mandarins* (New York: Pantheon, 1969), 27.

11. See, for example, Zhang Shanyu, "Lun renkou heli zaifenbu" (On rational population redistribution), *Renkou yu jingji* (Population and economy), 3 (1995), 3–9.

12. Wolfgang Franke, *The Reform and Abolition of the Traditional Chinese Examination System* (Cambridge, Mass.: Harvard University East Asian Monographs, 1968); for the text of the 1905 abolition proposal, see Zhu Shoupeng, comp., *Shierchao Donghua lu: Guangxu chao* (Donghua Gate records of the Guangxu reign), (Taibei: Wenhai 1963 ed.), 9: 5372–5375; G. R. Searle, *The Quest for National Efficiency: A Study in British Politics and Political Thought, 1899–1914* (Oxford: Blackwell, 1971), 57–58.

13. Yang Bingjie, "Zhongguo gongwuyuan zhiwei fenlei: ershi shiji sanshi niandai de yichang zhenglun" (China's 1930s-era debate about the classification of civil service positions), *Shehui kexue* (Social sciences), 5 (2004), 101–108.

14. Pham Quynh, "Chan chinh quan truong" (The improvement of officialdom), *Nam phong* (The southern ethos), March (1926), 108–112.

15. Hans Rogger, "Americanism and the Economic Development of Russia," *Comparative Studies in Society and History,* 23 (July 1981), 382–420.

16. *Xinhua yuebao* (New China monthly report), 1996, 10: 42–43; Xiong Zijian, *Dangdai Zhongguo sichao shuping* (A review of thought trends in contemporary China), (Taibei: Wenjin chubanshe, 1992), 29–37; Liu Yongji, *Zhongguo guan wenhua pipan* (A critique of Chinese bureaucratic culture), (Beijing: Zhongguo jingji chubanshe, 2000), 253–254; Nguyen Duc Uy in *Nhan dan,* Jan. 6, 1977, 5.

17. Mark Mazower, *Dark Continent: Europe's Twentieth Century* (New York: Knopf, 1999), 79.

1. Questioning Mandarins

1. Felipe Fernandez-Armesto, *Millennium: A History of the Last Thousand Years* (New York: Touchstone, 1995), 11.

2. Immanuel Wallerstein, *The Essential Wallerstein* (New York: The New Press, 2000), 454–471.

3. Harold Perkin, *The Third Revolution: Professional Elites in the Modern World* (London: Routledge, 1996), 1, 9–11.

4. Richard Pipes, "Max Weber and Russia," *World Politics,* 7 (April 1955), 371–401.

5. Lu Shiyi, *Sibianlu jiyao* (Summary version of the Chronicles of careful thought and clear distinctions), 18:1, in Tang Shouqi, comp., *Lu Futing xiansheng yishu* (The bequeathed works of Lu Shiyi), (Beijing: n.p., 1900).

6. Peter H. Lee, ed., *Sourcebook of Korean Civilization* (New York: Columbia University Press, 1996), 25–29; Phan Huy Chu, *Lich trieu hien chuong loai chi* (A

classified treatise of the institutions of successive courts), (Hanoi: Su hoc, 1962 ed.), III: 26: 19.

7. Le Quy Don, *Van dai loai ngu* (Classified discourse from the library), (Hanoi: Van hoa, 1961 ed.), II: 110–111.

8. Xu Songtao, *Zhongguo gongwuyuan zhidu* (The Chinese civil servants system), (Hong Kong: Shangwu, 1997), 2–3.

9. Min Jiayin, "Xitong kexue he shengtai wenming" (The system sciences and ecological civilization), *Weilai yu fazhan* (Future and development), 6 (1998), 31–33.

10. Philip A. Kuhn, *Origins of the Modern Chinese State* (Stanford: Stanford University Press, 2002), 2, 92.

11. He Qinglian, "Zhongguo gaige de lishi fangwei" (The historical compass bearings of the Chinese reforms), in Liu Zhifeng, comp., *Zhongguo zhengzhi tizhi gaige wenti baogao* (Reports on the problem of Chinese political system reforms), (Beijing: Zhongguo dianying, 1999), 3–26.

12. Chai-sik Chung, "Changing Korean Perceptions of Japan on the Eve of Modern Transformation," *Korean Studies*, 19 (1995), 39–50; Huynh Sanh Thong, *The Heritage of Vietnamese Poetry: An Anthology* (New Haven: Yale University Press, 1979), 31–36.

13. Ni Shui, "Tu guan shuo" (On indigenous minority officials), in He Changling, comp., *Huangchao jingshi wenbian* (A compilation of statecraft essays of the present court), (Taibei: Wenhai, 1972 ed.), 86: 1b–2; Sheng Kang, comp., *Huangchao jingshi wenbian xubian* (A compilation of statecraft essays of the present court, continued), (Taibei: Wenhai, 1972 ed.), 66: 55–58b.

14. *Dai Nam thuc luc chinh bien* (Primary compilation, the veritable records of the imperial south), (Hue: 1821 and thereafter), 2, 194: 36; 2, 40: 10.

15. James B. Palais, *Politics and Policy in Traditional Korea* (Cambridge, Mass.: Harvard Council on East Asian Studies and Harvard University Press, 1991), 12, 114, 312; B. A. Elman and A. Woodside, eds., *Education and Society in Late Imperial China, 1600–1900* (Berkeley: University of California Press, 1994), 465, 526.

16. A 1994 poll of young adults in Beijing and Seoul, conducted by a Chinese futurological society, asked them a classic Confucian question: Should oldest sons live with their parents even after the sons have married? Only 19.3 percent of the Beijing Chinese polled, but 50.4 percent of the Seoul Koreans, said yes. *Shehuixue yanjiu* (Sociological research), 2 (1996), 72–81.

17. Palais, *Politics and Policy in Traditional Korea*, 4–6.

18. Do Thai Dong, "Co cau xa hoi—van hoa o Mien Nam nhin theo muc tieu phat trien cua Ca Nuoc" (The south's sociocultural structure from the vantage point of the whole country's development goals), *Xa hoi hoc* (Sociology), 1 (1991), 10–14.

19. Alexander Woodside, "Territorial Order and Collective Identity Tensions in Confucian Asia: China, Vietnam, Korea," *Daedalus,* Summer (1998), 191–220.

20. He Zhongli, "Ershi shiji de Zhongguo keju zhidu shi yanjiu" (Twentieth-century studies about the history of the Chinese civil service examination system), *Lishi yanjiu* (Historical research), 6 (2000), 142–155. Benjamin A. Elman, *A Cultural History of Civil Examinations in Late Imperial China* (Berkeley: University of California Press, 2000), is an excellent Western account.

21. Henry Kammen, *Early Modern European Society* (London: Routledge, 2000), 71–73, 93–94.

22. M. I. Finley, *Democracy Ancient and Modern* (London: Hogarth Press, 1985), 87–88.

23. Lee, *Sourcebook of Korean Civilization,* 33–36.

24. Martina Deuchler, *The Confucian Transformation of Korea: A Study of Society and Ideology* (Cambridge, Mass.: Harvard Council on East Asian Studies and Harvard University Press, 1992), 292–295.

25. James B. Palais, "A Search for Korean Uniqueness," *Harvard Journal of Asiatic Studies,* 55, 2 (1995), 409–425; Lee, *Sourcebook of Korean Civilization,* 185–188.

26. Phan Ngoc Lien et al., "Hoi thao: Nhan thuc ve moi quan he lich su Viet-Nam—Nhat Ban" (Conference discussions: Recognitions of Vietnam-Japan historical relations), *Nghien cuu lich su* (Historical research), 2 (1998), 92–96.

27. Herman Ooms, *Tokugawa Ideology: Early Constructs, 1570–1680* (Princeton: Princeton University Press, 1985), 171.

28. Phan Huy Chu, *Lich trieu hien chuong loai chi* (A classified treatise of the institutions of successive courts), (Hanoi: Su hoc, 1962 ed.), II: 19: 98–102.

29. Helga Nowotny, *Time: The Modern and Postmodern Experience* (Cambridge: Polity Press, 1994), trans. Neville Plaice, 16.

30. For example, Nguyen Hong Phong, "Co mot tam hon Viet-Nam" (There is a Vietnamese soul), *To quoc* (Ancestral land), January (1971), 14–16.

31. Nowotny, *Time,* 7.

32. Sebastian Conrad, "What Time Is Japan? Problems of Comparative (Intercultural) Historiography," *History and Theory,* 1 (1999), 67–83.

33. Dominic Lieven, *The Aristocracy in Europe 1815–1914* (New York: Columbia University Press, 1992), 219.

34. Max Weber, *The Religion of China* (New York: Free Press, 1951), trans. Hans H. Gerth, 115, 128.

35. Ding Shouhe, comp., *Zhongguo lidai zhiguo ce xuancui* (Selected highlights of Chinese state administration policies through the centuries), (Beijing: Gaodeng jiaoyu, 1994), 206–210.

36. Georges Benko and Ulf Strohmayer, eds., *Space and Social Theory: Interpreting Modernity and Postmodernity* (Oxford: Blackwell, 1997), 2.

37. Jian Bozan, comp., *Wuxu bianfa* (The reforms of 1898), (Shanghai: Renmin, 1957), 2: 175–176.

38. William A. Green, "Periodizing World History," *History and Theory*, 34, 2 (1995), 99–111; Umberto Eco et al., *Conversations about the End of Time* (London: Penguin, 2000), trans. I. Maclean and R. Pearson, 186.

39. In his closing address to a political conference in March 2000, the Chinese politburo member Li Ruihuan pointedly counted the number of references to time in the second and third volumes of Deng Xiaoping's selected writings (153 of 179 selections allegedly alluded to it); said that the misuse of even fragments of time could lead to exponential increases in historical backwardness; and attributed the pathologies of the actors in the Chinese political system (overstaffing, "blind" policymaking, meaningless jurisdictional disputes, and drunkenness and debauchery) to "unhealthy" attitudes to time. *Xinhua yuebao*, 4 (2000): 85–87.

40. Conrad, "What Time Is Japan?," 67–83.

41. Michael Mann, *The Sources of Social Power* (Cambridge: Cambridge University Press, 1986), 1: 524; William H. McNeill, *The Global Condition* (Princeton: Princeton University Press, 1992), 147–148.

42. R. Bin Wong, *China Transformed: Historical Change and the Limits of European Experience* (Ithaca: Cornell University Press, 1997), 2, 202, 282.

43. Wang Boxin, "He cai" (Investigating capacity), in Sheng, *Huangchao jingshi wenbian xubian*, 15: 3–4.

2. Meritocracy's Underworlds

1. Jacob Burckhardt, *The Civilization of the Renaissance in Italy* (London: Allen and Unwin, n.d.), trans. S. G. C. Middlemore, 41, 54–55, 188, 227–228, 261, 266; Roberta Garner, "Jacob Burckhardt as a Theorist of Modernity," *Sociological Theory*, 8, 1 (Spring 1990), 48–84.

2. Xiong Mingan, *Zhongguo gaodeng jiaoyu shi* (A history of Chinese high-level education), (Chongqing: Chongqing chubanshe, 1983), 17.

3. Anthony Giddens, *The Consequences of Modernity* (Stanford: Stanford University Press, 1990); Huang Ping, "Cong Xiandaixing dao "Di Santiao Daolu': Xiandaixing zhaji zhi yi" (From modernity to 'the third way': One reading note on modernity), *Shehuixue yanjiu* (Sociological Research), 3 (2000), 26–44.

4. Immanuel Wallerstein, *The Essential Wallerstein* (New York: The New Press, 2000), 347–348.

5. Blaise Pascal, *Pensées* (London: Penguin, 1966), trans. A. J. Krailsheimer, 54 (5:94).

6. Peter H. Lee and Wm. T. deBary, eds., *Sources of Korean Tradition* (New York: Columbia University Press, 1997), 1: 150; Hoa Bang, "Cao Ba Quat voi cuoc khoi nghia chong trieu Nguyen 1854–1856" (Cao Ba Quat and the uprising against the Nguyen court 1854–1856), *Nghien cuu lich su* (Historical research), 121 (April 1969), 27–40.

7. Alasdair MacIntyre, "Ideology, Social Science, and Revolution," *Comparative Politics*, 5 (April 1973), 321–342.

8. Ding Shouhe, comp., *Zhongguo lidai zhiguo ce xuancui* (Selected highlights of Chinese state administration policies through the centuries), (Beijing: Gaodeng jiaoyu, 1994), 363–368.

9. Peter H. Lee, ed., *Sourcebook of Korean Civilization* (New York: Columbia University Press, 1996), 15–21; Le Quy Don, *Quan thu khao bien* (An examination and discussion of the many books), (Hanoi: Khoa hoc xa hoi, 1995 ed.), 420.

10. Yuan Mei, *Xiaocang shan fang shiwen ji* (Collected poetry and prose of the Small Granary Hill Studio), (Shanghai: Guji, 1988 ed.), 2: 1593–1595.

11. Ernest Gellner, *Plough, Sword, and Book: The Structure of Human History* (London: Paladin, 1991), 193–204.

12. Pierre Bourdieu, *Language and Symbolic Power* (Cambridge, Mass.: Harvard University Press, 1991), trans. G. Raymond and M. Adamson, 43.

13. Lee and deBary, *Sources of Korean Tradition*, 1: 274–276; Wang Boxin, "Wang Yan" (The words of the king), in Sheng Kang, comp., *Huangchao jingshi wenbian xubian* (A continued compilation of the statecraft essays of the present court), (Taibei: Wenhai, 1972 ed.), 10: 3–4.

14. Bernard S. Cohn, *Colonialism and Its Forms of Knowledge: The British in India* (Princeton: Princeton University Press, 1996); Christopher A. Bayly, *Empire and Information: Intelligence Gathering and Social Communication in India, 1780–1870* (Cambridge: Cambridge University Press, 1996).

15. Le Quy Don, *Kien van tieu luc* (A small chronicle of things seen and heard), (Hanoi: Khoa hoc xa hoi, 1977 ed.), 113–114; *Da Qing Gaozong Chunhuangdi shilu* (Veritable records of the Qianlong reign), (Tokyo: Okura shuppan kabushiki, 1937), 963: 14–15b; Lee, *Sourcebook of Korean Civilization*, 21–25.

16. Wang Boxin, "He cai" (Investigating capacity), in Sheng, *Huangchao jingshi wenbian xubian*, 15: 3–4.

17. Ding Shouhe, *Zhongguo lidai zhiguo ce xuancui*, 371–377.

18. Gu Yanwu, "Feng lu" (Official salaries), in Gu Yanwu, *Rizhilu jishi* (The chronicles of daily knowledge and collected commentaries), (Changsha: Yuelu Shushe, 1994 ed.), comp. Huang Rucheng, 438–441.

19. Guo Chengkang, "18 shiji houqi Zhongguo tanwu wenti yanjiu" (A study of the Chinese corruption problem in the second half of the eighteenth century), *Qingshi yanjiu* (Research in Qing history), 1 (1995), 13–26.

20. Fang Junyi, "Shili shiyi shuo" (On hereditary clerks and hereditary office servants), in Sheng, *Huangchao jingshi wenbian xubian*, 28: 29–30.

21. Ki-baik Lee, *A New History of Korea* (Cambridge, Mass.: Harvard University Press, 1984), trans. E. W. Wagner, 256; Phan Huy Chu, *Lich trieu hien chuong loai chi* (A classified treatise of the institutions of successive courts), (Hanoi: Su hoc, 1962 ed.), II: 19: 88; William T. Rowe, *Saving the World: Chen Hongmou and Elite Consciousness in Eighteenth-century China* (Stanford: Stanford

University Press, 2001), 339–344; Chen Hongmou, *Zaiguan fajie lu* (Chronicles of bureaucratic laws and precepts about what to avoid), preface, 1–2b, in Chen Hongmou, *Wuzhong yigui* (Five sourcebooks), (Shanghai: Zhonghua Shuju, 1936 ed.).

22. *Da Qing Gaozong Chunhuangdi shilu,* 745: 17b–19b.

23. Lu Yitong, "Xuli lun" (On sub-official functionaries), in Sheng, *Huangchao jingshi wenbian xubian,* 28: 4–13.

24. Michael Mann, *The Sources of Social Power* (Cambridge: Cambridge University Press, 1986), 1: 524; William McNeill, *The Global Condition* (Princeton: Princeton University Press, 1992), 148.

25. For example, Zhang Lüxiang, *Xunzi yu* (Discourses of instruction for children), 2: 25b, in Zhang Lüxiang, *Zhang Yangyuan jishu* (Collected writings of Zhang Lüxiang), (N.p.: Jiangsu shuju, 1871 ed.).

26. Zhao Yi, "Ming biansheng gongjiao bingshu zuiduo" (On the supreme numerousness of border province attack troops in the Ming), in He Changling, comp., *Huangchao jingshi wenbian* (A compilation of statecraft essays of the present court), (Taibei: Wenhai, 1972 ed.), 71: 7b-8.

27. Fang Zongcheng, "Xu Zhennü lun, shang," (A continued discussion of virtuous daughters, part one), in Sheng, *Huangchao jingshi wenbian xubian,* 69: 23–24.

28. Susan Mann, "Grooming a Daughter for Marriage: Brides and Wives in the Mid-Ch'ing Period," in R. S. Watson and P. B. Ebrey, eds., *Marriage and Inequality in Chinese Society* (Berkeley: University of California Press, 1991), 205.

29. Conrad Totman, *Early Modern Japan* (Berkeley: University of California Press, 1993), 286; Zhu Shoupeng, comp., *Shierchao Donghua lu: Guangxu chao* (Donghua Gate records of the Guangxu reign), (Taibei: Wenhai, 1963 ed.), 10: 5712–5713.

30. Yu Yingshi, *Zhongguo sixiang chuantong de xiandai quanshi* (A contemporary exegesis of Chinese intellectual tradition), (Taibei: Lianjing, 1987), 35.

31. Cao Xuan Huy et al., comp., *Tuyen tap tho van Ngo Thi Nham* (Selected works of prose and poetry of Ngo Thi Nham), (Hanoi: Khoa hoc Xa hoi, 1978), 2: 103–109.

3 .Administrative Welfare Dreams

1. R. Bin Wong, *China Transformed: Historical Change and the Limits of European Experience* (Ithaca: Cornell University Press, 1997), 98–99.

2. Christian Bay, *The Structure of Freedom* (Stanford: Stanford University Press, 1958), 4–5.

3. Ki-baik Lee, *A New History of Korea* (Cambridge, Mass.: Harvard University Press, 1984), trans. E. W. Wagner, 224–225.

4. Peter H. Lee and Wm. T. deBary, eds., *Sources of Korean Tradition* (New York:

Columbia University Press, 1997), 1: 328–329; Wang Chengbo and Sun Wenxue, *Zhongguo fushui sixiang shi* (A history of Chinese thought about taxes), (Beijing: Zhongguo caizheng jingji, 1995), 217–220; Alexander Woodside, *Vietnam and the Chinese Model* (Cambridge, Mass.: Harvard Council on East Asian Studies and Harvard University Press, 1988), 221; James B. Palais, *Confucian Statecraft and Korean Institutions* (Seattle: University of Washington Press, 1996), 277, 311.

5. Jean-Pierre Gutton, *La Société et Les Pauvres en Europe* (Paris: Presses Universitaires de France, 1974), 94; Bronislaw Geremek, *Poverty: A History* (Oxford: Blackwell, 1994), trans. A. Kolakowska, 20, 188–189.

6. Anthony Grafton, "Humanism and Political Theory," in J. H. Burns, ed., *The Cambridge History of Political Thought 1450–1700* (Cambridge: Cambridge University Press, 1991), 10.

7. Thomas Hobbes, *Behemoth or The Long Parliament* (Chicago: University of Chicago Press, 1990 ed.), ed. F. Tönnies, 40, 56.

8. Wang and Sun, *Zhongguo fushui sixiang shi*, 517–518.

9. C. B. A. Behrens, *Society, Government, and the Enlightenment: The Experience of Eighteenth-Century France and Prussia* (New York: Harper and Row, 1985), 78–88.

10. William H. McNeill, *The Global Condition* (Princeton: Princeton University Press, 1992), 106–108.

11. Tang Chenglie, "Zhi fu bian er" (Administering the primary tax, part two), and Tang Chenglie, "Guochao fuyi zhi zhi xu" (Preface to The system of taxes and labor services of the present court), both in Sheng Kang, comp., *Huangchao jingshi wenbian xubian* (A continued compilation of the statecraft essays of the present court), (Taibei: Wenhai, 1972 ed.), 34: 3–4b, 19–21.

12. To borrow the language of William Gamble, "The Middle Kingdom Runs Dry: Tax Evasion in China," *Foreign Affairs,* November-December (2000), 16–20.

13. Wu Shichang, "Cong Zhongguo de lishi kan minzhu zhengzhi" (A look at democratic government from the perspective of Chinese history), in Liu Zhifeng, comp., *Zhongguo zhengzhi tizhi gaige wenti baogao* (Reports on the problems of Chinese government reforms), (Beijing: Zhongguo dianying, 1999), 425–429.

14. Karl Mannheim, *Ideology and Utopia* (New York: Harcourt Brace and World Harvest Books, 1936), trans. L. Wirth and E. Shils, 118–119.

15. Philip Kuhn, "Ideas behind China's Modern State," *Harvard Journal of Asiatic Studies,* 55, 2 (1995), 295–337.

16. Gu Yanwu, "Junxian lun" (On prefectures and counties), in Gu Yanwu, *Gu Tinglin xiansheng yishu* (The bequeathed works of Gu Yanwu), (Taibei: Jinxue shuju, 1969 ed.), 2: 778–790.

17. Tony Judt, *A Grand Illusion? An Essay on Europe* (New York: Hill and Wang, 1996), 118–119.

18. Wang Huizu, *Xuezhi yishuo* (Opinions about learning to govern), (Changsha: Commercial Press, 1939 ed.), 1: 11–12.

19. E. J. Dionne, Jr., *Why Americans Hate Politics* (New York: Simon and Schuster, 1991).

20. Judt, *A Grand Illusion,* 118–121.

21. A. Woodside, "The Ch'ien-lung Reign," in Denis Twitchett and Willard Peterson, eds., *The Cambridge History of China,* vol. 9A (Cambridge: Cambridge University Press, forthcoming).

22. Woodside, "The Ch'ien-lung Reign."

23. Qin Huitian, "Juanjian jianshou yingu shu" (Memorial proposing the combined collection of silver and grain in the contributions to purchase imperial college degrees), in He Changling, comp., *Huangchao jingshi wenbian* (Compilation of statecraft essays of the present court), (Taibei: Wenhai, 1972 ed.), 39: 12b-13b.

24. Palais, *Confucian Statecraft and Korean Institutions,* 1000.

25. Phan Huy Chu, *Lich trieu hien chuong loai chi* (A classified treatise of the institutions of successive courts), (Hanoi: Su hoc, 1962 ed.), III: 29: 57–71.

26. Peter H. Lee, ed., *Sourcebook of Korean Civilization* (New York: Columbia University Press, 1996), 46–71.

27. Wei Yuan, "Lujiang Zhangshi yizhuang ji" (An account of the charitable estate of the Zhang lineage of Lujiang), in He Changling, *Huangchao jingshi wenbian,* 58: 10b-11; for Xie Jieshu, see Zhao Jing and Yi Menghong, comp., *Zhongguo jindai jingji sixiang ziliao xuanji* (A selection of materials on modern Chinese economic thought), (Beijing: Zhonghua Shuju, 1982), 1: 154–168.

28. Martina Deuchler, "The Practice of Confucianism: Ritual and Order in Choson Dynasty Korea," in Benjamin Elman, H. Ooms, and J. Duncan, eds., *Rethinking Confucianism* (Los Angeles: UCLA Asian Pacific Monograph Series, 2002), 292–334; Vu Duy Men and Bui Xuan Dinh, "Huong Uoc: khoan uoc trong lang xa" (Village covenants: Deeded covenants in the villages), *Nghien cuu lich su* (Historical research), 7–8 (1982), 43–49. See also Martin Grossheim, "Village Laws (Huong Uoc) as a Source for Vietnamese Studies," in P. LeFailler and J. M. Mancini, eds., *Viet Nam: Sources et Approches* (Aix-en-Provence: Publications de l'Université de Provence, 1996), 103–123.

29. Monika Ubelhör, "The Community Compact of the Sung and Its Educational Significance," in Wm. T. deBary and John W. Chaffee, eds., *Neo-Confucian Education: The Formative Stage* (Berkeley: University of California Press, 1989), 371–388.

30. Charles Taylor, "Modes of Civil Society," *Public Culture,* 3, 1 (1990), 95–118.

31. Ki-baik Lee, *A New History of Korea,* 206–207; Peter Lee, *Sourcebook of Korean Civilization,* 162–177.

32. A. Woodside, "Classical Primordialism and the Historical Agendas of Vietnamese Confucianism," in Elman, Ooms, and Duncan, *Rethinking Confucian-*

ism, 116–143; Vu Duy Men and Bui Xuan Dinh, *Nghien cuu lich su,* 7–8 (1982), 43–49.

33. Wing-tsit Chan, trans., *Instructions for Practical Living and Other Neo-Confucian Writings by Wang Yang-ming* (New York: Columbia University Press, 1962), 298–306.

34. Phan Huy Chu, *Lich trieu hien chuong loai chi,* III: 29: 70–71.

35. *Da Qing Gaozong Chunhuangdi shilu* (Veritable records of the Qianlong reign), (Tokyo: Okura shuppan kabushiki, 1937), 201: 2b-3b; 1143: 29–31b.

36. Nguyen Khac Vien's two-part essay appears in *Nhan dan,* 6–7 September 1988, 3. See the useful note on his life by Dan Duffy in *Vietnam Forum,* 15 (1996), 185–186.

37. Amartya Sen, *Poverty and Famines: An Essay on Entitlement and Deprivation* (Oxford: Clarendon Press, 1981), 1–4, 166.

4. Management Theory Mandarins?

1. Liang Qichao, "Xuexiao zonglun" (A general discussion of schools), in Shu Xincheng, comp., *Jindai Zhongguo jiaoyu shi ziliao* (Materials about modern Chinese educational history), (Beijing: Renmin Jiaoyu, 1962 ed.), 3: 936–944.

2. Geremie R. Barmé, *In the Red: On Contemporary Chinese Culture* (New York: Columbia University Press, 1999), 265–268.

3. Zhang Pingzhi and Yang Jinglong, *Zhongguo ren de maobing* (The defects of Chinese people), (Beijing: Zhongguo Shehui, 1998), 88–90; Liu Yongji, *Zhongguo guan wenhua pipan* (A criticism of Chinese bureaucrat culture), (Beijing: Zhongguo jingji, 2000), 42, 457.

4. *Xinhua yuebao,* 2 (2001), 145–146.

5. Dao Phan, *Ho Chi Minh: danh nhan van hoa* (Ho Chi Minh: Cultural celebrity), (Hanoi: Van Hoa, 1991).

6. Dam Van Chi, *Lich su van hoa Viet-Nam: Sinh hoat tri thuc ky nguyen 1427–1802* (A history of Vietnamese culture: Intellectual life of the era 1427–1802), (Ho Chi Minh City: Tre, 1992), 5; Nguyen The Long in *Nhan dan chu nhat,* August 29, 1993, 5.

7. *Xinhua yuebao,* 7 (1987), 5–12; Xiang Hong, comp., *Rencaixue cidian* (A dictionary of people of talent studies), (Chengdu: Chengdu keji daxue, 1987), 98–103; He Zhongli, "Ershi shiji de Zhongguo keju zhidu shi yanjiu" (Twentieth-century studies about the history of the Chinese civil service examination system), *Lishi yanjiu* (Historical research), 6 (2000), 142–155.

8. Hu Sheng, *Hu Sheng wenji 1979–1994* (The writings of Hu Sheng, 1979–1994), (Beijing: Zhongguo Shehui Kexue, 1994), 489–497.

9. Interview with Song Defu in *Xinhua yuebao,* 9 (2000), 137–138.

10. *Xinhua yuebao,* 9 (2000), 78–79.

11. Zhang Zhihao, "Jiakuai ganbu renshi zhidu gaige de zhanlüe yiyi ji mianlin wenti" (The strategic significance of accelerating cadre personnel system reform and the problems it faces), *Shehui kexue* (Social sciences), 4 (2001), 5–9.

12. Guo Xiaojun, "Woguo lingdao kexue lilun yanjiu de yibu lizuo" (A powerful work of our country's theoretical research in leadership science), *Weilai yu fazhan* (Future and development), 5 (1999), 53: Sheldon S. Wolin, *Politics and Vision: Continuity and Innovation in Western Political Thought* (Boston: Little, Brown, 1960), 376–381.

13. Peter M. Senge, *The Fifth Discipline: The Art and Practice of the Learning Organization* (New York: Currency Doubleday, 1990) xv, 3–4; Ma Hong, "Qiye guanli de xin fazhan" (New developments of business management), *Zhongguo gongye jingji* (Chinese industrial economy), 1 (1999), 59–64.

14. Han Jun, "Guanyu nongcun jiti jingji yu hezuo jingji de ruogan lilun yu zhengce wenti" (Some theoretical and government policy problems concerning the rural collective economy and cooperative economy), *Zhongguo nongcun jingji* (Chinese village economy), 12 (1998), 11–19, 17.

15. Diep Van Son, "Ban ve van de cong chuc Viet-Nam" (On the problem of Vietnamese state officials), *Nha nuoc va phap luat* (State and law), 3, (1995), 7–13.

16. Liu Guoguang, *Zhongguo jingji tizhi gaige de moshi yanjiu* (A study of the models of reform of the Chinese economic system), (Beijing: Zhongguo Shehui Kexue, 1988), 56–57.

17. Dao Tri Uc, "Nen hanh chinh Viet-Nam trong qua trinh doi moi kinh te va chinh tri" (Vietnamese administration in the process of economic and political renovation), *Nha nuoc va phap luat*, 3 (1992), 33–41.

18. Peter Gay, *The Enlightenment: An Interpretation* (New York: Norton, 1969), 2: 24.

19. Lu Zhongwei, *Xinjiu jiaoti de Dong Ya geju* (The East Asian pattern of the new replacing the old), (Beijing: Shishi, 1993); He Peizhong, "Zhong-Ri-Han sanguo zhongqingnian weilai yishi diaocha fenxi" (Analysis of a survey of the consciousness of the future of middle-aged and young people in the three countries of China, Japan, and South Korea), *Shehuixue yanjiu* (Sociological research), 2 (1996), 72–81, 80.

20. Phan Cong Nghia et al., "Thuc trang doi ngu can bo quan ly kinh te vi mo o cac co quan trung uong" (The actual situation of the ranks of macroeconomic management cadres in central agencies), *Nghien cuu kinh te* (Economic research), 12 (1997), 31–38: Tran Anh Tho in *Nhan dan chu nhat*, September 26, 1993, 6.

21. Wu Xinye, "Hanguo gongwuyuan kaoshi zhidu ji qi dui Zhongguo de jidian qishi" (The South Korean civil service examination system and its points of enlightenment with respect to China), *Dong bei Ya luntan* (Northeast Asia forum), 2 (1998), 42–45.

22. Atul Kohli, "Where Do High Growth Political Economies Come From? The Japanese Lineage of Korea's Developmental State," in Meredith Woo-Cumings, ed., *The Developmental State* (Ithaca: Cornell University Press, 1999), 93–136.

23. Wu Xinye, "Hanguo gongwuyuan kaoshi zhidu," 42–45.

24. Song Defu in *Xinhua yuebao,* 8 (1993), 40–42; Nguyen Thy Son, "Dao tao nghe quan ly va lanh dao" (Training the profession of management and leadership), *Tap chi cong san* (The Communist Journal), 6 (1998), 33–45,43.

25. D. W. Y. Kwok, *Scientism in Chinese Thought 1900–1950* (New Haven: Yale University Press, 1965), 3.

26. H. Lyman Miller, *Science and Dissent in Post-Mao China: The Politics of Knowledge* (Seattle: University of Washington Press, 1996), 256–260; Peter R. Moody, Jr., "The Political Culture of Chinese Students and Intellectuals: A Historical Examination," *Asian Survey,* 28, 11 (November 1988), 1140–1160.

27. Xiao Feng, "Zhongguo jishu fazhan de xianzhuang yu dongli fenxi" (An analysis of the present circumstances and impetus of Chinese technological development), *Weilai yu fazhan,* 4 (2000), 17–22; Merle Goldman and Roderick MacFarquhar, "Dynamic Economy, Declining Party State," in Goldman and MacFarquhar, eds., *The Paradox of China's Post-Mao Reforms* (Cambridge, Mass.: Harvard University Press, 1999), 3–29, 9.

28. *Xinhua yuebao,* 9 (1999), 83–86.

29. Luo Renshan, "Shanghai gongchandangyuan jiazhi quxiang bianhua tedian yanjiu" (A study of the peculiarities of the value orientation changes of Shanghai Communist Party members), *Shehui kexue,* 12 (2000), 15–19.

30. Perry Link, *Evening Chats in Beijing: Probing China's Predicament* (New York: Norton, 1992), 67.

31. Zhang Yueming, "Zhishi jingji shidai dui siwei fangshi de yaoqiu" (The demands of the knowledge economy age on modes of thought), *Shehui kexue,* 6 (2000), 35–38.

32. Wang Chuanshi, "Nongye tidu jishu de xuanze yu zhuanyi" (The selection and transfer of agricultural graded techniques), *Zhongguo nongcun jingji,* 7 (2001), 10–14.

33. Phan Cong Nghia, "Thuc trang doi ngu can bo quan ly kinh te vi mo," *Nghien cuu kinh te,* 12 (1997), 31–38.

34. Rudolf G. Wagner, "Lobby Literature: The Archaeology and Present Functions of Science Fiction in China," in Jeffrey C. Kinkley, ed., *After Mao: Chinese Literature and Society, 1978–1981* (Cambridge, Mass.: Harvard University Press, 1985), 17–62, 22, 35.

35. Ding Shouhe, comp., *Zhongguo lidai zhiguo ce xuancui* (Selected highlights of Chinese state administration policies through the centuries), (Beijing: Gaodeng Jiaoyu, 1994), 363–368; Cao Xuan Huy and Thach Can, comp., *Tuyen tap*

tho van Ngo Thi Nham (Selected works of prose and poetry of Ngo Thi Nham), (Hanoi: Khoa Hoc Xa Hoi, 1978), 2: 236–243.

36. Fan Ping, in Han Mingmo et al., *Zhongguo shehui yu xiandaihua* (Chinese society and modernization), (Beijing: Zhongguo Shehui, 1998), 236–243.

37. Zhang Zhuoyuan, "Gaige kaifang yilai woguo jingji lilun yanjiu de huigu yu zhangwang" (A review of our country's economic theory research since the reforms opening, and a look ahead), *Jingji yanjiu* (Economic research), 6 (1997), 7–8.

38. Huang Xumin, "Qian tan Ruxue chuantong de weilaiguan yu siwei dingshi" (Simple talk about Confucian literati learning's traditional view of the future and established thinking tendencies), *Weilai yu fazhan* (Future and development), 3 (1997), 62–64.

39. Phan Dinh Dieu, "Dieu khien hoc" (Cybernetics), *Nhan dan,* October 21, 1973, 2; Tran Duc Qui, "Mot so y kien ve cong tac du bao" (Some opinions on forecasting work), *Tap chi hoat dong khoa hoc* (Journal of scientific activities), 6 (1973), 1–3.

40. Yu Guangyuan, comp., *Zhongguo lilun jingjixue shi 1949–1989* (A history of Chinese theoretical economics, 1949–1989), (Zhengzhou: Henan Renmin, 1996), 829–834; Wei Hongsen, *Xiandai kexue jishu de fazhan yu kexue fangfa* (The development of contemporary science and technology and science methods), (Beijing: Qinghua Daxue, 1985), 47–66; Kang Rongping et al., "Xiandai xitonglun de ruogan lishi wenti" (Some historical questions of contemporary systems theory), *Shehui kexue jikan* (Social sciences journal), 4 (1984), 32–37.

41. Zhang Wei, *Renkou kongzhixue* (Population control studies), (Beijing: Zhongguo Renkou, 2000), 49–51.

42. Elizabeth J. Perry, "Crime, Corruption, and Contention," in Goldman and MacFarquhar, *The Paradox of China's Post-Mao Reforms,* 322, 434.

43. Tyrene White, "Domination, Resistance, and Accommodation in China's One-child Campaign," in E. J. Perry and Mark Selden, eds., *Chinese Society: Change, Conflict, and Resistance* (London: Routledge, 2000), 102–119.

44. James Z. Lee and Wang Feng, *One Quarter of Humanity: Malthusian Mythology and Chinese Realities* (Cambridge, Mass.: Harvard University Press, 1999), 21.

45. Ellen Chesler, *Woman of Valor: Margaret Sanger and the Birth Control Movement in America* (New York: Simon and Schuster, 1992), 85–87, 194–195, 245–246; Wang Qisheng, "Jindai Zhongguo jieyu yundong shulue" (A brief account of the modern Chinese birth control movement), *Renkou yanjiu* (Population research), 5 (1990), 48–50.

46. Zhang Fusheng, "Shitan minguo shiqi renkou sixiang de heli chengfen" (Exploring the rational composition of republican period population thought), *Renkou yu jingji* (Population and economy), 2 (1996), 58–61.

47. Su Ronggua, "Guanyu renkou jihua de lilun he shijian wenti de tantao" (An in-

quiry into problems of theory and practice related to population planning), *Renkou yanjiu,* 5 (1995), 8–12.

48. Dennis Hodgson, "Demography as Social Science and Policy Science," *Population and Development Review,* 9 (March 1983), 1–34.

49. Wang Shengjin and Li Guofu, "Dong Bei Ya diqu de renkou zhuanhuan yu kaifa" (Demographic transition and development in the Northeast Asia region), *Dong Bei Ya luntan,* 3 (1997), 16–19.

50. For example, Tham Vinh Hoa (Shen Ronghua) et al., *Ton trong tri thuc, ton trong nhan tai: ke lon tram nam chan hung dat nuoc* (Respect intellectuals, respect people of talent: A great plan of a hundred years for restoring the country), (Hanoi: Chinh tri Quoc gia, 1996), trans. Nguyen Nhu Diem, originally a Shanghai Chinese publication.

51. Charles Hirschman et al., "Vietnamese Casualties during the American War: A New Estimate," *Population and Development Review,* 21 (December 1995), 783–812; Daniel Goodkind, "Rising Gender Inequality in Vietnam since Reunification," *Pacific Affairs,* 68 (Fall 1995), 342–359; Daniel Goodkind, "Vietnam's One-or-two-child Policy in Action," *Population and Development Review,* 21 (March 1995), 85–111.

52. Zha Ruichuan, "Jin yibu you de fangshidi yanjiu woguo renkuo wenti" (Researching our country's population problem from a better vantage point), *Renkou yanjiu,* 5 (1995), 1–7.

53. Dai Xingyi, "Woguo renkou rongliang wenti xinyi" (New views about the problem of our country's population capacity), *Shehui kexue,* 2 (1991), 37–40.

54. Son Nam, "Nhung anh huong cua ton giao va tin nguong dan gian Nam bo doi voi ke hoach hoa gia dinh" (The influences of southern religions and popular beliefs with respect to family planning), *Xa hoi hoc* (Sociology), 2 (1990), 55–60.

55. Nguyen The Hue, "Vai y kien ve dan so va chinh sach dan so o cac cong dong dan toc Viet-Nam hien nay" (Some opinions on population and population policy in Vietnam's ethnic communities at present), *Tap chi dan toc hoc* (Journal of ethnology), 1 (1993), 33–40.

56. Harold Perkin, *The Third Revolution: Professional Elites in the Modern World* (London: Routledge, 1996), 218. Sheng Hong, *Jingjixue jingshen* (The spirit of economics), (Guangzhou Guangdong Jingji, 1999), 143–144. For more on Sheng Hong, see Joseph Fewsmith, *China since Tiananmen: The Politics of Transition* (Cambridge: Cambridge University Press, 2001), 81–82, 109–110.

Conclusion

1. Do Muoi, in *Tap chi cong san,* 1 (1992), 10–17.
2. See the brilliant discussion of this in Jeffrey C. Kinkley, *Chinese Justice, The Fiction* (Stanford: Stanford University Press, 2000), 269–282.

3. Reprinted in *Xinhua yuebao,* 8 (2000), 119–120.

4. Bruce Cumings, *North Korea* (New York: The New Press, 2004), 128.

5. Peter H. Lee, ed., *Sourcebook of Korean Civilization* (New York: Columbia University Press, 1996), 34–36; Mark Setton, *Chong Yagyong: Korea's Challenges to Orthodox Neo-Confucianism* (Albany: SUNY Press, 1997).

6. Gu Yanwu, *Rizhilu jishi* (The chronicles of daily knowledge and collected commentaries), comp. Huang Rucheng (Changsha: Yuelu Shushe, 1994 ed.), 327.

7. Le Quy Don, *Van dai loai ngu* (Classified discourse from the library), (Hanoi: Van Hoa, 1961 ed.), 1: 235–236.

8. Hu Xu, "Qing boju xiaodi shu" (Memorial requesting the broad recommendation of filial sons and devoted brothers), in He Changling, comp., *Huangchao jingshi wenbian* (Compilation of statecraft essays of the present court), (Taibei: Wenhai, 1972 ed.), 57: 15–15b.

9. Wang Chunbo, "Ruhe pojie 'Huang Zongxi dinglü'" (How to analyze and solve the Huang Zongxi law), *Nongye jingji wenti* (Issues in agricultural economy), 11 (2004), 4–8. See also Wm. Theodore deBary, *Waiting for the Dawn: A Plan for the Prince* (New York: Columbia University Press, 1993), 128–138; and Lee, *Sourcebook of Korean Civilization,* 211–214.

10. Le Quy Don, *Kien van tieu luc* (A small chronicle of things seen and heard), (Hanoi: Khoa hoc Xa hoi, 1977 ed.), 121–122.

11. Jiao Xun, *Diaogu lou ji* (The Diaogu Mansion literary collection), (N.p., 1824 ed.), 12: 12b-14b.

12. Phan Huy Chu, *Lich trieu hien chuong loai chi* (A classified treatise of the institutions of successive courts), (Hanoi: Su Hoc, 1962 ed.), III: 29: 47–48.

13. Bertrand Russell, *The Problem of China* (London: Allen and Unwin, 1922), 10, 214.

14. Walter Benjamin, *Illuminations* (New York: Schocken, 1969), trans. Harry Zohn, 257; William H. McNeill, *The Global Condition* (Princeton: Princeton University Press, 1992), 148.

Index

Administrative Efficiency Research Society
(*Xingzheng xiaolü yanjiu hui*), 12
Appanage lands, 48–49
Aristocracy: vs. bureaucracy, 1–2, 5, 8, 13–
14, 18–19, 20, 26–31, 38–39, 46–47, 51,
54–55, 74, 75, 83, 108–111, 115; in China,
22, 26, 27, 33–34, 51, 53, 54; in Korea,
27–29, 49, 50, 60, 68, 70, 87–88, 114; in
Vietnam, 28–31; in Europe, 32, 34, 48, 60,
115. *See also* Feudalism
Aristotle, 60; on slavery, 28
Arnold, Matthew, 17
Association of Southeast Asian Nations
(ASEAN), 87
Australia, 102
Austro-Hungarian Empire, 6

Bacon, Francis, 34–35
Barmé, Geremie: on self-loathing in China,
79
Barnard, Chester, 14
Bell Telephone Co., 96
Benjamin, Walter, 115
Benko, Georges, 34
Berlin, Isaiah, 107
Berman, Harold J., 4, 15
Bertalanffy, Ludwig von, 95
Binet, Alfred, 10
Bourdieu, Pierre, 44
Buddhism, 15, 24, 104
Burckhardt, Jacob, 55; on modernity and
the Renaissance, 38
Bureaucracy: vs. aristocracy, 1–2, 5, 8, 13–
14, 18–20, 26–31, 38–39, 46–47, 51, 54–
55, 74, 75, 83, 108–111, 115; vs.
Confucian family hierarchy, 2–3, 52–53;
and morality, 3, 7–8, 13, 19–20, 42–43,

47–48, 52–54, 64–65, 75, 76, 80, 84, 105–
106, 110–111, 113–114; Weber on, 5, 18–
19, 32–33; vs. feudalism, 5–6, 8, 10, 19,
23–24, 26–27, 31, 38–39, 49–51, 52, 54–
55, 58, 64–66, 69, 70–72, 74, 83, 108–109,
111; and local conditions, 5–6, 57, 63–76,
84–86, 93–94, 96, 98–100, 102–106, 112–
113, 115; relations with hereditary
monarchs, 6, 44–45, 55, 56, 74–75, 78–79,
109, 110, 115; self-esteem of officials, 7,
8, 46–52, 75, 83, 108, 110–111;
bureaucratic accountability paradox, 7,
110–111; conversion of political
problems into administrative concerns,
8–9, 41, 45, 58–60, 64, 75, 86, 89, 97–98;
bureaucratic subjectivity, 9, 20, 69, 77–
78, 93–94, 97, 102–105, 110, 113; and
collective purposes, 10–11; salary levels,
11, 12, 30, 47–49, 51; work classification,
11, 12, 88; and Taylorism, 11–12; and
rationality, 14, 54–55, 57, 62–64, 67, 86–
87, 97–98, 103; evaluations by superiors,
17; unintended consequences of policies,
20, 63, 98; promotion/demotion, 30;
corruption, 30, 36–37, 47–48, 80, 110,
112; tests of bureaucratic performance,
30–31; time-based performance criteria,
30–31; Sima Guang on, 41–42, 93, 94,
110; short-term appointments, 42; and
public good, 42–44; factionalism in, 42–
44, 61; mediation of disputes by, 43–46,
60, 85–86, 90–91; goal displacement in,
51–52; relations between higher and
lower officials, 51–52, 68, 113; and
mobilization of people, 52–55; "ten
thousand capabilities" views of, 77–78
Burke, Edmund, 34, 109

135

Business schools, Western: management theory in, 13, 78, 96, 107; attitudes toward east Asian mandarinates in, 78, 83–84, 86

Cai Yuanpei, 99
Capitalism: and modernity, 1, 4, 9, 15, 18, 36, 56–57; globalization, 9, 83, 108; and meritocracy, 39; risk in, 39, 76, 92, 115; invisible hand of the market, 43; and welfare state, 56–57; and contraception, 99
Chams, 24, 28
Charlemagne, 4
Chen Changheng, 99
Chen Hongmou, 50–51, 52, 112
Cheng Duanli, 82
China: Tang dynasty, 1–2, 4, 24–26, 33, 37, 42, 48, 49, 51, 58, 61–63, 66–67, 69–70, 71, 85, 89; civil service examinations (imperial), 1–2, 5, 6, 8, 10–11, 13–14, 17, 19, 22, 26–27, 32–34, 40, 46–47, 50–51, 53, 115; Confucianism, 3, 13–14, 17, 22–23, 43, 44, 47, 53–54, 71–74, 82, 83, 91, 94–95, 111; feudalism, 4–6, 33–34, 38, 53–54, 57, 58, 65, 70–71, 114; Ming dynasty, 5, 7, 27, 29, 45, 49, 114; vs. Korea, 5, 8, 15–16, 21–31, 33, 38–39, 40, 42, 44–46, 49–51, 53, 56–59, 67–69, 71–73, 83, 109, 114; Northern Wei dynasty, 5, 58; vs. Austria-Hungary, 6; Qianlong emperor, 6, 67, 74–75; clerks (*xuli*), 7, 49–52, 67, 112, 113; vs. Vietnam, 8, 9, 15, 21–31, 33, 38–40, 42, 44–46, 48–51, 53, 56–59, 67–69, 71–73, 77, 80, 82–96, 101–105, 109, 112, 114; mountain people, 9; under Communism, 9, 13, 21, 77, 79–102, 107–108, 112–114; village covenants/community compacts, 9, 71–73; family planning programs, 9, 97–105, 107; Opium War, 10, 114; under Nationalists, 11–12; Taylorism in, 11–12; Guanzi, 13; Western management science in, 13; Han dynasty, 13, 24, 25, 30, 33, 45; Gansu, 22; Qing dynasty, 22, 23, 27, 29, 53, 54, 63, 68, 114; aristocracy, 22, 26, 27, 33–34, 51, 53, 54; ethnic minorities, 22, 32, 49, 53; relations with Korea, 24–25; relations with Vietnam, 24–25; court centralization, 25; government records and history, 25; law, 25; six specialized ministries, 25, 46; vs. Roman empire, 25–26; presented scholar degree, 26; Shandong, 26; political unification of, 27; Zhou dynasty, 27, 38, 40, 45, 58, 94; upward mobility, 33, 54; talent validation, 37; Wang Boxin on history of, 37; Shang dynasty, 40, 58, 94; Taiping rebellion, 40, 112; Song dynasty, 41–44, 47, 61, 71, 106; scholar-official factionalism, 42–44; office of censors, 45–46; corruption of officials, 47–48, 49; female fidelity, 53–54; attitudes toward Japan, 54, 86–87, 88, 101, 104; welfare strategies, 56, 58–59, 60, 67–68, 69–70, 74, 75, 76, 94–95, 100, 114; Xia dynasty, 58, 94; "equal-fields" system, 58–59, 61–62, 67–70, 74–75; "two taxes" law of 780 C.E., 61–63; taxes, 61–64, 67–69, 102; Yongzheng emperor, 63; popular apathy, 64–67, 71, 73; merchants, 67, 68, 74; market economy in, 77, 81, 83, 87, 94, 113; historical continuity, 77–78, 81–85; civil service examinations (contemporary), 78, 81, 82, 87–89; contemporary civil service system, 78, 81, 82, 88–90, 93–94; attitudes toward South Korea, 78, 85–89; self-loathing in, 79, 84–85; brain drain, 82–83; Shanghai, 83, 91; scientism, 89–95; Suzhou, 99; Western fictional heroes in, 107–108; Anhui province, 113; contemporary tax reform, 113–114
Chomsky, Noam, 8
Chong Tojon, 58
Chong Yagyong, 28, 69–70, 109, 113
Christina, Queen, 27
Chrysler Corp., 13
Chu, Phan Huy, 30, 50, 61, 74, 115
Cicero, Marcus Tullius, 44, 60
Civil service examinations: in imperial China, 1–2, 5, 6, 8, 10–11, 13–14, 17, 19, 22, 26–27, 32–34, 40, 46–47, 50–51, 53, 115; in imperial Korea, 2, 5, 8, 17, 19, 26–28, 40, 41, 46–47, 53, 72, 87–88, 109, 114; transparency in, 2–3; in imperial Vietnam, 2–3, 8, 12–13, 17, 19, 26–27, 29, 32, 40, 46–47, 53, 80, 114; relationship to

duties, 3, 17; writing style in, 6; and
depersonalized management, 8; grade
inflation in, 8, 19; east Asian criticisms
of, 19, 33, 46–47, 78–81, 102; and
presented scholar degree, 26; and
disadvantaged minorities, 32; rebellions
against, 40, 112; and self-esteem, 46–47,
75; eight-legged essay, 47; and political
loyalty, 52–54; and social welfare, 59–60;
and poverty, 59–60, 75; in South Korea,
78, 87–89; in contemporary China, 78,
81, 82, 87–89; as instrument of
despotism, 78–79; in contemporary
Vietnam, 81, 84, 87–89
Civil service pay levels, 11, 12, 30, 47–49, 51
Civil service work classifications, 11, 12, 88
Clerks (*xuli*), 7, 49–52, 56, 67, 112
Cocteau, Jean, 23
Collectivism, 77, 83, 84, 86
Colonialism: of France, 10, 12–13, 80; of
Britain, 10, 45; of Japan, 10, 78, 87–88
Communism: Vietnam under, 9, 13, 14, 75–
77, 80–96, 107; China under, 9, 13, 21, 77,
79–102, 107–108, 112–114
Comte, Auguste, 89
Confucianism: kinship hierarchy in, 2–3,
52–53, 91; morality and virtue in, 3, 7–8,
15, 19–20, 25, 47, 52–54, 111; in China, 3,
13–14, 17, 22–23, 43, 44, 47, 53–54, 71–
74, 82, 83, 91, 94–95, 111; in Vietnam, 3,
17, 19–23, 71–74, 80–81, 90, 95, 104, 111;
in Korea, 3, 17, 22–23, 28, 71–74, 109,
111; and village covenants, 9, 71, 72; in
Japan, 21; academies, 22–23; three bonds
in, 25; filial piety in, 52–53; Mencius, 59,
61, 63, 67, 74–76, 83, 111, 113
Conrad, Joseph, 41
Conrad, Sebastian, 31, 36
Constant, Benjamin, 37
Control theory (cybernetics), 9, 95–102
Corruption, 30, 36–37, 63, 80, 110, 112; in
China, 47–48, 49
Cybernetics (control theory), 9, 95–102
Czechoslovakia, 13

Dali, Salvador, 36
Democracy: as ideal, 22, 33, 114; in Athens,
23, 27, 36, 114; popular apathy in, 66, 67,
74; and famine, 76; public good in, 84

Demographers, Western, 100
Deng Xiaoping, 81, 101
Deuchler, Martina, 28
Dieu, Phan Dinh, 97
Doan Nhu Hai, 29
Don, Le Quy, 42, 90, 111, 114

Eco, Umberto, 35
Einstein, Albert, 83, 90
Enlightenment, 15, 20, 36, 82, 85, 112
Epistemological self-righteousness, 41, 49
Equality: Hayek on, 13–14; in Western
liberalism, 40; "equal-fields" system/
"well-field" system, 58–59, 60, 61–62, 67–
70, 74–75. *See also* Collectivism
Europe: vs. east Asia, 3, 6, 7, 9, 10, 11, 14,
17, 19, 20, 26–27, 31–33, 40, 41, 43–52,
54–57, 59–60, 62–66, 68, 71–74, 76, 86–
87, 106, 108–109; and modernity, 3–4,
34–36, 39, 115; meritocracy in, 7, 10;
Reformation, 7, 20, 41; feudalism, 10, 26–
27, 32, 33, 43, 57, 62, 70, 73, 108–109;
Renaissance, 15, 26, 34, 35, 38;
aristocracy, 32, 34, 48, 60, 115; papal
authority in, 43; kings in, 44–45; self-
esteem of bureaucrats in, 48; mass
education, 50; poverty, 59; tax immunity
in, 60, 62; political revolutions, 60, 62, 66,
77, 109; voter apathy, 66, 67; religious
wars, 66, 72, 73; civil society, 71–72;
welfare state, 76; agriculture, 92; fertility
rates, 100. *See also* Colonialism
European Union, 10, 27, 65, 66

Factionalism, official, 42–44, 61
Family planning programs: in Vietnam, 9,
97, 98, 101–102, 104–105; in China, 9,
97–105, 107; in India, 98; in Indonesia,
98; and Sanger, 98–99
Fan Zhongyan: on public servants, 106
Fayol, Henri, 107
Fernandez-Armesto, Felipe, 17
Feudalism: defined, 5; in Vietnam, 4–6, 8,
27–29, 31, 38, 48–50, 57; in Korea, 4–6, 8,
27–29, 31, 38, 41, 48–50, 57, 72, 108–109;
in China, 4–6, 33–34, 38, 53–54, 57, 58,
65, 70–71, 114; vs. bureaucracy, 5–6, 8,
10, 19, 23–24, 26–27, 31, 38–39, 49–52,
54–55, 58, 64–66, 69, 70–72, 74, 83, 108–

Feudalism *(continued)*
109, 111; in Europe, 10, 26–27, 32, 33, 43,
57, 62, 70, 73, 108–109; in Japan, 10, 29,
54; Gu Yanwu on, 64–65, 114. *See also*
Aristocracy
Fichte, Johann Gottlieb, 78
Ford Motor Co., 91
France: colonial policies, 10, 12–13, 80;
Franco-Prussian War, 11; French
revolution, 62, 66, 77, 109; feudalism in,
109
Frederick the Great, 62

Galileo Galilei, 18
General Motors, 91
Germany: under Wilhelm II, 5; after
Reformation, 7, 20; feudalism in, 32; civil
service in, 88
Giddens, Anthony: on science in
modernity, 39; on risk in modernity, 39,
76, 92–93, 115; *The Consequences of
Modernity,* 39, 92, 115
Globalization, 9, 83, 108
Goals: displacement of, 51–52, 56; as
professed, 56
Goldman, Emma, 99
Goodkind, Daniel, 102
Goya, Francisco, 86
Grafton, Anthony, 59
Great Britain: Levellers, 7; English
revolution, 7, 60; Labour Party, 10;
Opium War, 10, 114; civil service in, 11,
12, 14; colonial rule in India, 45; relations
with Prussia, 62; Anglicanism in
England, 66
Gu Yanwu, 79, 110; on corruption in
officials, 47–48, 49; on feudalism, 64–65,
114
Guizot, François, 3
Gunazi, 13
Guzong, 74–75

Haeju covenant, 72
Hauser, Philip, 100
Hayek, Friedrich von, 13–14
He Qinglian, 21
Hegel, G. W. F., 61, 81
Heine, Heinrich, 78
Hmong, 104–105

Ho Chi Minh, 80–81
Hobbes, Thomas, 44, 60, 66
Holy Roman Empire, 26
Holmes, Sherlock, 108
Hong Kong, 101
Hong Kyongnae, 40
Hu Jun, 62
Hu Sheng, 81–82, 84
Hu Xu, 111–112
Hu Yaobang, 81, 82, 84
Huang Ping, 39
Huang Zongxi, 55, 113, 114
Huboldt, Wilhelm von, 17
Hui of Liang, King, 76

Iacocca, Lee, 13, 107
India: British colonialism in, 45; family
planning programs in, 98
Individualism, 35, 37, 70
Indonesia, family planning programs in, 98
Industrialization, 1, 4, 15, 36, 115
Information theory, 89, 95
IQ tests, 47
Italy, 15, 35, 38
Ito Hirobumi, 88

James I, 26–27
Japan: feudalism, 10, 29, 54; colonialism, 10,
78, 87–88; Russo-Japanese War, 11;
Confucianism, 21; civil service, 21, 88;
Tokugawa shoguns, 29; Conrad on, 31,
36; Prince Saionji, 54; merchants, 68;
influence in contemporary China and
Vietnam, 86–87, 88, 104; fertility rates,
101
Jiang Zemin, 80
Jiangxi covenant of 1520, 73–74
Jiao Xun, 114

Kang Youwei, 34
Kant, Immanuel, 33, 78
Kantorowicz, Ernst, 32–33
Khmers, 24, 28
Korea: Choson dynasty, 1, 22–23, 27–29,
44–45, 69–70, 72–73, 114; Koryo dynasty,
1, 25, 40; civil service examinations
(imperial), 2, 5, 8, 17, 19, 26–28, 40, 41,
46–47, 53, 72, 87–88, 109, 114;
Confucianism, 3, 17, 22–23, 28, 71–74,

109, 111; feudalism, 4–6, 8, 27–29, 31, 38, 41, 48–50, 57, 72, 108–109; vs. China, 5, 8, 15–16, 21–31, 33, 38–40, 42, 44–46, 49–51, 53, 56, 57–59, 67–68, 69, 71–73, 83, 109, 114; village covenants/ community compacts, 9, 71, 72; vs. Vietnam, 15, 16, 21–31, 33, 38–40, 42, 44–46, 48–51, 53, 56–60, 69–73, 83, 109, 110, 114; relations with China, 24–25; court centralization, 25; government records and history, 25; law, 25; six specialized ministries, 25; presented scholar degree, 26; *yangban* elite, 27–29, 49, 50, 60, 68, 70, 87–88, 114; aristocracy, 27–29, 49, 50, 60, 68, 70, 87–88, 114; slavery in, 28; upward mobility in, 33; scholar-official factionalism, 42, 44; office of censors, 45, 46; corruption of officials, 49; clerks (*sori*) in, 49, 50; King Taejo, 56; Taewongun, 56; welfare strategies, 56–59, 67–70; *Taedongbop* (Great Uniformity Law), 57–58; taxes, 57–58, 60, 69–70; Agency to Bestow Blessings (*Sonhyech'ong*), 58; "equal-fields" system, 58–59, 67–68, 74, 75; land reform, 69–70; *Sirhak* reformers, 70; civil service examinations (South Korea), 78, 87–89; Silla, 88
Kuhn, Philip, 21, 64–65
Kuroda Toshio, 100–101
Kwok, D. W. Y., 90

Lai, Tuong, 93
Land reform, 8–9, 56, 58–59, 67, 68, 69–70, 74
Lao, the, 28
Latour, Bruno, 4
Lenin, V. I., 13, 43, 77, 83, 85, 95
Le Quy Don, 19–20
Li Anshi, 58
Liang Qichao, 78–79
Liberty, human, 20; and modernity, 18, 100, 102; ancient vs. modern, 37; in Western liberalism, 40; Rousseau on, 68; and contraception, 98–99, 107
Liji (Record of Rituals), 58
Limited terms of office, 17
Lincoln, Abraham, 83
Link, Perry, 91

Locke, John, 41, 44; *The Reasonableness of Christianity,* 43
Loyalty, political, 52–55
Loyseau, Charles, 109
Lu Shiyi, 19
Lu Xun, 14
Lü Family community compact, 71
Luther, Martin, 7, 20
Ly, Ho Quy, 56

Macartney, Lord, 29
Machiavelli, Nicolò: on meritocracy, 7, 39–40
MacIntyre, Alasdair, 41
Malthus, Thomas, 98
Mann, Michael, 52
Mann, Susan, 53–54
Mannheim, Karl: *Ideology and Utopia,* 64, 86, 89, 98
Mao Zedong, 74, 80, 83, 85, 96, 101
Maria Theresa, 6
Marx, Karl, 4
Mass nationalism, 8, 10, 11, 52, 66, 77
Mazarin, Jules, Cardinal, 33
McNeill, William, 52, 62, 115
Mencius, 83, 111; on poverty, 59, 61, 63, 74–76; on tax rates, 61, 67, 113; confrontations with King Hui of Liang, 76
Meritocracy: vs. aristocracy, 1–2, 13–14, 20, 23–24, 27–31, 36–37, 39–41, 110–111; hazards of, 7, 8, 39–55, 88–89; in Europe, 7, 10; Machiavelli on, 7, 39–40; Pascal on, 7, 39–41, 43, 46, 111; opposition to, 8; and corruption, 30, 36–37, 47–48; debates in China on, 33–34, 49–51, 79, 85, 88–89, 109–112, 114–115; Wang Boxin on, 37; relationship to capitalism, 39; Wallerstein on, 39–40; definitions of merit, 39–40, 45–46, 50, 109–110; and hereditary monarchy, 55; Hu Xu on, 111–112
Microsoft, 83
Modernity: rationalization processes in, 1, 4, 5, 9, 11–12, 15, 18, 38, 63, 82–84, 86–87, 90, 95–96, 107; and capitalism, 1, 4, 9, 15, 18, 36, 56–57; and industrialization, 1, 4, 15, 36, 115; and Eurocentrism, 3–4, 34–36, 39, 115; Latour on, 4; and

Modernity *(continued)*
    technology, 18, 34–35, 100, 102, 115;
    Wallerstein on, 18, 39–40, 100, 102; and
    human liberation, 18, 100, 102; Perkins
    on, 18, 105; and time, 31–36, 55, 76;
    Benko on, 34; and science, 34–35, 39, 82;
    Eco on, 35; Burckhardt on, 38; progress
    in, 38; and risk expansion, 39, 76, 92,
    115; Giddens on, 39, 76, 92–93, 115; and
    mediation of disputes, 42–44; McNeill
    on, 62, 115; and solidarity deficits, 70;
    and civil society, 71–72; and fertility
    rates, 98, 99, 100–101
Muoi, Do, 107
Mussolini, Benito, 15

Napoleon I, 77, 83
Nham, Ngo Thi, 55, 93
North Korea, 77, 112
Nozick, Robert: on justice, 44

Office of censors: in Korea, 45, 46; in China,
    45–46; in Vietnam, 45–46, 85
Ogyū Sorai, 54
Opium War, 10, 114
Ortai, 55
Orwell, George, 110

Pak Chega, 19
Palais, James, 23, 58, 68
Park Chung Hee, 87
Pascal, Blaise: on meritocracy, 7, 39–40, 41,
    43, 46, 111
Patriotism, 8, 10; and education, 11
People of talent, 46–47, 52, 55, 81–84, 101,
    108
Perkins, Harold: on modernity, 18, 105
Pierre de Blois, 59
Pipes, Richard, 18–19
Plato, 60
Pluralism, 3
Political science, 13
Popper, Karl, 107
Popular apathy, 9, 60, 103; in China, 64–67,
    71, 73; Wang Huizu on, 65, 67; in
    democracy, 66, 67, 74
Poverty, 8–9, 58; Mencius on, 59, 61, 63,
    74–76; as politically created, 59, 61, 63–
    64, 67, 69, 74–76; Qin Huitian on, 67

Prussia: Franco-Prussian War, 11; Frederick
    the Great, 62; bureaucracy, 64, 88;
    relations with Great Britain, 62;
    Protestantism in, 66
Public good, 42–44, 84

Qian Duansheng, 12
Qian Xuesen, 96
Qianlong emperor, 6, 67, 74–75
Qin Huitian, 67
Quat, Cao Ba, 40

Rationalization processes, 6–7, 14, 54–55,
    97–98, 115; in modernity, 1, 4, 5, 9, 11–
    12, 15, 18, 38, 63, 82–84, 86–87, 90, 95–
    96, 107; Weber on, 5, 63, 86; Taylorism,
    11–12, 13, 83, 90, 95–96, 107
Rawls, John, 107; on justice, 44
Reformation, 7, 20, 41
Renaissance, 15, 26, 34, 35, 38
Richelieu, Cardinal, 33
Risk in capitalism, 39, 76, 92, 115
Ritual conditioning processes, 15
Roman empire, 25–26; law in, 36
Roman republic, 60
Rousseau, Jean-Jacques, 43; on freedom, 68
Rumania, 13
Russell, Bertrand: *The Problem of China*,
    115

Saionji, Prince, 54
Salt and iron debate, 13
Sanger, Margaret, 98–99, 107
Science: and modernity, 34–35, 39, 82;
    social science vs. social engineering, 57,
    100; information science, 89; worship of,
    89–95, 100; role in mediation, 90–91
Self-esteem of officials, 7, 8, 46–52, 75, 83,
    108, 110–111
Self-restraint of officials, 105–106
Sen, Amartya, 76
Seneca, 60
Senge, Peter: *The Fifth Discipline*, 83–84
Sheng Hong: on self-restraint, 105–106
Siam, 22; feudalism in, 10
Sima Guang, 41–42, 93, 94, 110
Simon, Herbert, 107
Singapore, 101
Six specialized ministries, 25, 29, 33

Slavery: Aristotle on, 28; in Korea, 28
Social classes, 39, 58–59, 92–93, 108–109; social mobility, 33, 54
Social science vs. social engineering, 57, 100
Solidarity deficits, 66, 70–74, 114
South Korea, 101; civil service examinations in, 78, 87–89; influence in China and Vietnam, 85–89
Spain, 5
Stalin, Joseph, 13, 75
State salvationism, 35, 57, 58, 61, 68, 70, 94–95. *See also* Welfare strategies
Suharto, 98
Sun Yat-Sen, 79
Sunzi, 83
Sweden, 27
Systems theory/engineering, 9, 20, 95–102, 103

Taejo, King, 56
Taewongun, 56
Tai, the, 28
Taiping rebellion, 40, 112
Taiwan, 13–14
Tang, King, 40
Tang Bin, 52
Taxes: Zhu Xi on scholarly skills and, 17; in Vietnam, 22, 60–61, 68–70; *Taedongbop* (Great Uniformity Law), 57–58; in Korea, 57–58, 60, 69–70; tax reforms, 57–58, 60–67, 97–98, 102, 113–114; ten percent tax, 61; Wang Fuzhi on, 61; Ye Shi on, 61; Mencius on, 61, 67, 113; "ten thousand capabilities" (*wen neng*) view of, 61, 70, 85; land-labor-household tax, 61–62, 69; "two taxes" law of 780 C.E., 61–63; Yang Yan's reforms, 61–63, 66–67, 102; in China, 61–64, 67–69, 102; money vs. kind payment, 62; Huang Zongxi on, 113, 114; in contemporary vs. imperial China, 113–114
Taylor, Frederick Winslow, 11–12, 13, 83, 90, 95–96, 107
Tay-son emperor, 73
Technology, 18, 34–35, 90, 100, 102, 115
Thorndike, Edward, 10
"Three dynasties" ideal: "well-field" system, 58, 60, 69–70, 74, 75; and welfare strategies, 58–59, 60, 69–70, 74, 75, 76, 94–95, 100, 114
Time: bureaucratic performance based on, 30–31; historical time, 31–36, 55, 76; short-term bureaucratic appointments, 42
Tocqueville, Alexis de, 3
Toffler, Alvin, 107
Toynbee, Arnold, 14
Trai, Nguyen, 80–81
Trinh lords, 29, 68–69
Tru, Nguyen Cong, 80
Ts'ui Liang, 5
Tu-duc, 56

Ubelhör, Monika, 71
Uc, Dao Tri, 85–86, 89
UNESCO, 80
United Nations, 102
United States: PhD training in, 3; civil service, 11, 12, 88; Supreme Court, 43; social philosophy in, 44; agriculture, 92; management theory in, 96

Vien, Nguyen Khac, 75
Vietnam: Nguyen dynasty, 1; Tran dynasty, 1; Le dynasty, 1, 25, 29; Ly dynasty, 1, 56; civil service examinations (imperial), 2–3, 8, 12–13, 17, 19, 26–27, 29, 32, 40, 46–47, 53, 80, 114; Confucianism, 3, 17, 19–23, 71–74, 80–81, 90, 95, 104, 111; feudalism, 4–6, 8, 27–29, 31, 38, 48–50, 57; vs. China, 8, 9, 15, 21–31, 33, 38–40, 42, 44–46, 48–51, 53, 56–59, 67–69, 71–73, 77, 80, 82–96, 101–105, 109, 112, 114; under Communism, 9, 13, 14, 75–77, 80–83, 84–95, 96, 107; village covenants/community compacts, 9, 71–73; family planning programs, 9, 97, 98, 101–102, 104–105; French colonial policies, 12–13, 80; vs. Korea, 15, 16, 21–31, 33, 38–40, 42, 44–46, 48–51, 53, 56–60, 69–73, 83, 109, 110, 114; ethnic minorities, 22, 24, 104–105; taxes, 22, 60–61, 68–70; assimilation in, 24; Da Nang, 24; Hue, 24; place names in, 24; relations with China, 24–25; court centralization, 25; government records and history, 25; law, 25; six specialized ministries, 25, 29;

Vietnam *(continued)*
  Ho Chi Minh City/Saigon, 25, 83;
  presented scholar degree, 26; aristocracy,
  28–31; Nguyen lords, 29; regional lords,
  29; Trinh lords, 29, 68–69; tests of
  bureaucratic performance, 30–31;
  upward mobility in, 33; scholar-official
  factionalism, 42; office of censors, 45–46,
  85; Cochinchina, 48; clerks (*tu lai*) in, 49,
  50; Tu-duc, 56; welfare strategies, 56, 58–
  59, 67–70, 74, 75; Binh Dinh province,
  58; "equal-fields" system, 58–59, 67–69,
  74, 75; merchants, 68; Tay-son emperor,
  73; agriculture, 75–76; market economy
  in, 77, 87; historical continuity, 77–78,
  80–81, 82, 85–89; contemporary civil
  service system, 81, 82–83, 87–89, 90, 93–
  94; civil service examinations
  (contemporary), 81, 84, 87–89; brain
  drain in, 82–83; attitudes toward South
  Korea, 85–89; attitudes toward Japan, 86–
  87, 88, 104; scientism, 89–95; Mekong
  delta, 104; Taoism, 104; Catholicism, 105
Village covenants/community compacts: in
  Korea, 9, 71, 72; in China, 9, 71, 72, 73; in
  Vietnam, 9, 71, 72–73
Voltaire, 50, 86

Wallerstein, Immanuel: on modernity, 18,
  39–40, 100, 102; on meritocracy, 39–40
Wang Anshi, 26; on corruption in office, 47
Wang Boxin, 37
Wang Fuzhi: on taxes, 61, 85
Wang Huachen, 97
Wang Huizu, 105; *Xuezhi yishuo,* 14–15; on
  popular apathy, 65, 67
Wang Mingsheng, 23
Wang Yangming, 73–74
Webb, Sidney and Beatrice, 11
Weber, Max, 4, 14; on bureaucracy, 5, 18–
  19, 32–33, 63; on Germany, 5, 32; on
  rationalization, 5, 63, 86; on east Asian
  mandarinates, 32–33
Wei Yuan, 70–71
Welfare strategies: land reform, 8–9, 56, 58–
  59, 67–70, 74; as state salvationism, 35,
  57, 58, 61, 68, 70, 94–95; in Korea, 56,
  57–59, 67–70; in China, 56, 58–59, 60,

67–70, 74–76, 94–95, 100, 114; in
  Vietnam, 56, 58–59, 67–70, 74, 75;
  Taedongbop (Great Uniformity Law), 57–
  58; and "three dynasties" ideal, 58–60,
  69–70, 74–76, 94–95, 100, 114; "equal-
  fields" system, 58–59, 61–62, 67–70, 74
White, Tyrene, 98
Wiener, Norbert, 95, 96, 97, 106, 107
Wolsey, Thomas Cardinal, 33
Wong, R. Bin, 36, 56
World War One, 66, 78, 101
Written texts: and meritocracy, 8, 41; vs.
  direct/practical experience, 20–21, 34, 37,
  41–42, 44, 75, 82, 93, 95, 97, 102, 110;
  Sima Guang on, 41–42; and words of the
  king, 44–45
Wu, King, 40
Wu Jingzi, 112
Wu (Tang empress), 26

Xie Bokang: *Renshi xingzheng dagang,* 12
Xu Guangqi, 5

Yan Jiaqi, 4
Yang, Frank, 91
Yang Yan, 61–63, 66–67, 68, 102
Ye Shi: "The Man Who Flies to Pluto," 61
Ye Yonglie, 93
Yi I, 72
Yi Ik, 5, 28, 42
Yi Songgya, 56
Yongzheng emperor, 63
Yu Guangyuan, 96
Yu Hyongwon, 69
Yu Suwon, 46, 110
Yuan Mei: on scholar-officials of Song
  dynasty, 42–44; on mediation of disputes,
  43–44, 60
Yuan Shikai, 11
Yugoslavia, 13

Zha Ruichuan, 103
Zhang Juzheng, 63
Zhenning Yang, 91
Zhou li (Rituals of Zhou), 25, 38, 50
Zhu Rongji, 13
Zhu Xi, 17
Zuo Zongtang, 22